跨文化交际过程中的
语用失误研究

A STUDY OF PRAGMATIC FAILURE IN
CROSS-CULTURAL COMMUNICATION

尹丕安 著

西北工业大学出版社

西安

【内容简介】 本书以高等院校非英语专业学生为研究对象,探讨了在跨文化交际过程中,非英语专业学生语用失误产生的成因和规避策略。全书采取定性与定量研究相结合的方法,分三个部分系统地阐述了跨文化交际能力和跨文化语用能力之间的关系,以及跨文化语用能力的培养途径问题,主要从三方面进行阐述:一是语用观对跨文化交际的阐述;二是语用失误问题的实验研究;三是跨文化语用能力的培养。

本书的研究内容可供高等院校英语专业学生阅读及参考。

图书在版编目(CIP)数据

跨文化交际过程中的语用失误研究/尹丕安著.—
西安:西北工业大学出版社,2019.3
ISBN 978 - 7 - 5612 - 6331 - 0

Ⅰ.①跨… Ⅱ.①尹… Ⅲ.①文化交流-语用学-研究 Ⅳ.①G115 ②H0

中国版本图书馆 CIP 数据核字(2019)第 052247 号

KUAWENHUA JIAOJI GUOCHENG ZHONG DE YUYONG SHIWU YANJIU
跨 文 化 交 际 过 程 中 的 语 用 失 误 研 究

责任编辑:杨 睿   策划编辑:杨 睿
责任校对:朱辰浩   装帧设计:李 飞
出版发行:西北工业大学出版社
通信地址:西安市友谊西路 127 号   邮编:710072
电   话:(029)88491757,88493844
网   址:www.nwpup.com
印 刷 者:陕西向阳印务有限公司
开   本:727 mm×960 mm   1/16
印   张:7.875
字   数:154 千字
版   次:2019 年 3 月第 1 版   2019 年 3 月第 1 次印刷
定   价:33.00 元

如有印装问题请与出版社联系调换

Preface

With the increasing communication occurring across cultural boundaries understanding language use is becoming more and more important. The effectiveness and attainment of intercultural communication has become people's primary concern. However, not all the intercultrural communication proceeds as smoothly and successfully as people expect. Because of the difference between Chinese culture and English culture, pragmatic failures are more often than not experienced by the Chinese EFL learners.

Pragmatic failure is one of the most important aspects of the ineffectiveness of intercultural communication. This book makes a theoretical analysis of some common pragmatic failures caused by the Chinese EFL learners from the perspective of both intercultural communicative theory and pragmatic theory. What is more, a test and a questionnaire are conducted among the Chinese EFL students in order to probe into the essence of pragmatic failures. It is revealed that two types of pragmatic failures, namely, pragmalinguistic failures and sociopragmatic failures are equally made by the EFL learners. One's linguistic competence is not in positive proportion to his pragmatic competence. The issues raised in this book are clearly of vital importance for those trying to achieve effective communication.

In light of the above arguments and analysis, the author puts forward some suggestions about and approaches to the cultivation of pragmatic competence among the Chinese EFL learners and presents some tentative ideas on how to avoid pragmatic failures in intercultural communication.

Lastly, the author concludes that successful communication requires not just a high level of linguistic competence, but also a corresponding level of pragmatic competence. Both teachers and learners should focus on the two points: understanding the connotation of intercultural pragmatic competence; adopting peculiar teaching methodology, which may facilitate the improvement of learners' pragmatic competence.

Dut to the author's insufficient knowledge and horizon, it's inevitable to make some errors and mistakes. We are ready to welcome and accept all the suggestions and advices.

Author

2018 - 12

前　言

　　随着国际跨文化交际活动的日益增加,在不同的文化背景中如何利用语言进行交际正变得越来越重要。高效、成功地进行跨文化交际成为交际者关注的首要问题。然而,掌握了一门外语的语音、词汇和语法并不意味着能得心应手地利用该语言与说本族语者进行有效的交际活动。语言交际是语言因素与文化因素的融合与互动过程。由于文化背景不同,再加上各种语境因素的制约作用,跨文化交际活动并不像交际者所期望的那样能顺利进行。在这种情况下,语用失误便产生了。

　　语用失误是导致跨文化交际障碍的重要方面。它不是指一般的遣词造句中出现的语言运用错误,而是说话方式不妥,表达习惯不符合目标语文化,不能取得预期交际效果的失误。本书以中国高等院校非英语专业大学生为研究对象,对其在交际过程中出现的语用失误类型,运用语用学相关理论做了系统的分析。此外,为了进一步解析语用失误的本质,笔者以非英语专业大学生为测试和调查对象,对其进行了语用能力测试和问卷调查。结果表明:语用失误贯穿于跨文化交际过程的始终。语言语用失误和社交语用失误是最普遍的两种类型。该测试验证了笔者的假设:学习者(非英语专业大学生)的语法能力与其相应的语用能力不成正比。

　　由此可见,加强学习者语用能力的培养是解决跨文化交际过程中语用失误的关键,而这些问题的解决可从教学方法、教学大纲、课程设置、测试体系等方面进行改革。

　　要在跨文化交际过程中取得成功,交际者要同时具有较高的语法能力和语用能力。在外语学习和教学过程中,教师和学习者要充分认识以下两个重要因素,即学习者要充分理解跨文化语用能力的内涵;教师要尽可能采取有助于提高学习者语用能力的教学方法。只有这样,才能尽量避免语用失误的产生,促使跨文化交际活动顺利地进行。

由于笔者水平有限,一些错误和纰漏在所难免,敬请各位专家和读者批评指正。

著　者

2018 年 12 月

CONTENTS

目　　录

CHAPTER 1 INTRODUCTION

This chapter mainly focuses on the negative effect of pragmatic failures in communicative events as well as the importance of the study of pragmatic failures.

The use of language is greatly influenced by the cultural elements that attached to it. Language is inextricably tied to culture. Today's English is evidently turning into an international language, which implies that it has incorporated language cultural elements of various ethnic groups, and has become a language for intercultural communication. Through English, people of various cultures come to know other nations better. It is a remarkable fact that there are hundreds of times of many non-native English speakers in the world as native speakers. Therefore, when people use English as a medium of communication, their own culture often affect the second language. As a result, some common pragmatic errors come into being.

The cultural pragmatic differences between source language and target language are responsible for the pragmatic failures of various kinds in intercultural communication. The concept of "pragmatic failures" was proposed by Jenny Thomas in the early 1980's. According to Thomas, pragmatic failures fall into two categories: pragmalinguistic failures and sociopragmatic failures. Generally speaking, pragmalinguistic failures refer to the failure of language itself. It occurs when the interactor misuses the way of expression in the target language, or the interactor doesn't know the correct way of expression in the target language. It's mainly because they apply indiscriminately the semantic meaning and structure of the source language to that of the target language. Sociopragmatic failures result from the interactors misunderstanding of each other's cultural background. It is assumed that pragmalinguistic failures are connected with the learner's strategy of negative transference from the native language to the second language. Whereas sociopragmatic failures are closely tied to the social conditions of language use, for example, taboos, social norms, value judgment, etc.

Pragmatic failures occur throughout the process of intercultural communication. It is no point talking about pragmatic failures without mentioning cultural differences. Because of cultural differences, misunderstandings may take place, even if the speaker masters very well the pronunciation, grammar, vocabulary or idioms. In the course of intercultural communication, culture plays one of the most important roles. A Chinese EFL learner cannot hope to avoid pragmatic failure without some good background knowledge of the culture related to the target language. It is not a new idea that language and culture are inseparable. In this sense, the EFL learners are expected to learn the vocabulary and syntactic rules as well as the social rules of the foreign language.

In the process of intercultural communication, pragmatic failures occur so often that the necessity for attaching great importance to it is pressing. Thomas holds that pragmatic failures are caused by pragmatic transfer. That is, people from different cultural backgrounds directly translate their respective native language into the target language in communicating without considering the communicative rules these utterances should adhere to. Anthropologists hold that man is not only a social man, but also a cultured man. The Chinese like to greet each other by asking about the counterpart's personal business in many cases, whereas the English like to comment on the weather to start a conversation. These are the reflections of different cultures. The ignorance of cultural differences in the course of intercultural communication inevitably leads to the pragmatic transfer, thus causing pragmatic failures.

Thomas comments on the seriousness of pragmatic failures. According to her idea, grammatical failures may impede communication. But once the hearer is alert to the fact that the speaker is not fully grammatically competent, native speakers seem to have little difficulty in making allowances for it. But pragmatic failures are otherwise. If a non-native speaker appears to speak fluently, a native speaker is likely to attribute the apparent impoliteness not to any linguistic deficiency, but to boorishness or ill-will.

Theoretically speaking, pragmatic failures can be avoided. Firstly, the linguistic and cultural differences must be taken into account. Culture is multiple-dimensional, complex and all-pervasive. Language is one chief component of culture, and culture is much reflected through language. It is through language that we make contact with our surroundings and share with others our feelings. In interacting with others, an individual must attach great importance to the cultural difference between the source language and the target language. Since the target language opens a new world to him, many things are unfamiliar to him in his culture. Therefore, knowing something about the target culture is necessary for him to acquire real language competence, and thus avoiding pragmatic failures. Secondly, intercultural pragmatic competence, which differs from the general linguistic competence, must be highlighted. According to Chomsky, linguistic competence is the ability of an ideal native speaker to construct and recognize grammatical and only grammatical sentences in his language. Such competence is not adequate to enable him to use the language effectively, but rather, sometimes what is grammatical may not be acceptable and what is ungrammatical may not be inappropriate. Thus, it is evident that there are some other elements contributing to the linguistic competence in addition to the grammatical element. Under this circumstance, Hymes's concept of "communicative competence" comes to light, which is a complement to Chomsky's "linguistic competence" or "grammatical competence". After that, Widdowson brings forward the concept of "intercultural pragmatic competence". It contains two parts: the ability to identify the context under which an utterance is performed; the ability to understand the intended meaning of the speaker by that particular utterance. The cultivation and strengthening of pragmatic competence will pave the way for reducing the pragmatic failures in the course of intercultural communication.

In practice, the adjustment of China's EFL teaching system should be made. He Ziran argues that the learners' pragmatic competence couldn't be improved naturally in pace with the enhancement of their English grammatical ability. In classrooms, teachers may be successful in preparing the learners for communication in the foreign language by giving them insight and practice in grammatical structures. However, the exact nature of the communicative situations is highly unpredictable. Learners with a firm knowledge of grammar and a wide range of vocabulary are stuck in it and unable to carry out their communicative intent.

In this thesis, the author intends to demonstrate and analyze the causes and factors leading to pragmatic failures in the process ofintercultural communication. What is more, some strategies to avoid these failures are brought forward for the Chinese EFL learners. Through careful and intensive study, the author finds out that the Chinese EFL learners' intercultural pragmatic competence development has lagged behind or is overlooked to a large extent in contrast to their corresponding grammatical competence in EFL learning and teaching. To solve this problem, the author offers some suggestions about the cultivation of pragmatic competence in the course of EFL learning and teaching on the basis of some pedagogical principles.

This thesis is composed of six chapters. Chapter 1 briefly illustrates pragmatic failures as an obstacle to the achievement of intercultural communication and stresses the importance of the study and analysis of pragmatic failures.

In chapter 2, the author reviews some basic ideas in the field of intercultural communication in relation to pragmatics. Language, culture and communication are regarded as an interwoven system. Language is the common core of culture ingredients. Culture is much reflected through language. Culture is learned, acted out, transmitted and preserved through communication.

Communicative competence, intercultural communicative competence and pragmatic competence are three concepts proposed by Hymes and Widdowson. If EFL learners lay stress on their linguistic competence or grammatical competence, they may surely pay much attention to the accuracy of grammatical forms of language. If they take pragmatic competence as their chief target, attention to the "appropriateness" of language use will be paid in specific context to ensure that the purpose of communication can be achieved. What is more, the author maintains that cross-cultural awareness is essential to the reduction of pragmatic failures.

In chapter 3, some pragmatic theories associated with pragmatic failures are reviewed and analyzed, such as speech acts theory by Austin, indirect speech acts theory by Searle, the principle of cooperation by Grice, and the politeness principle by Leech and Gu Yueguo. In the meantime, the author cites many instances of pragmatic failures analyzed and interpreted by these theories. The author also centers on the pragmatic differences across language communication, which stem from the cultural diversity and have a direct impact on the miscommunication.

Chapter 4 is devoted to the pragmatic failures in intercultural communication. The author gives a detailed study on the pragmatic failures in terms of two categories, namely, pragmalinguistic failures and sociopragmatic failures, which is regarded as the nucleus of this thesis.

In order to reduce and avoid pragmatic failures, some measures and strategies must be taken to develop a learner's pragmatic competence. So chapter 5 of this papen is responsible for this aspect. To a large extent, the reduction and avoidance of pragmatic failures are associated with EFL learning and teaching. The author puts forward some suggestions about and approaches to the cultivation and improvement of EFL learners' pragmatic competence.

Eventually, the author draws a conclusion in the last chapter that pragmatic failures do exist all the way through the intercultural communication. A learner's linguistic competence is not in positive proportion to his corresponding pragmatic competence. It is expected that this thesis will draw both the EFL learners' and teachers' attention to the problems in pragmatic failures and that the objectives of intercultural communication will be better fulfilled.

第1章 引 言

本章主要介绍语用失误在跨文化交际中的不良影响,以及研究和分析语用失误的重要性。

文化因素在语言的使用中有极强的影响力,语言与文化密不可分。如今,英语作为一门国际性语言,不仅将各个国家的语言文化因素包含在内,而且成为一种跨文化交际工具。通过英语,不同文化背景的人可以对其他民族进行更好的了解。显然,世界上非英语母语的使用人数是英语母语使用人数的几百倍。因此,当人们采用英语作为交流媒介时,自身语言文化会影响到第二语言的使用。如此一来,就会产生语用失误。

源语和目标语之间的文化语用差异造成了在跨文化交际中出现各种语用失误。"语用失误"一词由 Jenny Thomas 在 20 世纪 80 年代早期所提出。根据 Thomas 所言,语用失误分为两类:语言语用失误和社交语用失误。一般而言,语言语用失误关乎语言自身层面,产生于使用者对目标语的错误表达,又或是使用者不了解正确的目标语表达方式。这主要是因为使用者将源语的语义和结构不加区别地应用在目标语之中。社交语用失误产生于双方在交流过程中,对彼此文化背景的误解。人们认为,语言语用失误和语言初学者对从母语到第二语言的负迁移学习策略有联系。然而,社交语用失误和社会环境下所使用的语言密切相关,例如,禁忌语、社会规范、价值判断,等等。

语用失误贯穿了整个跨文化交际过程,所以在讨论语用失误时,必然要提及文化的差异性。即使语言使用者能够很好地掌握发音、语法、词汇和习语,可是只要有文化差异的存在,使用中的失误就有可能发生。在跨文化交际过程中,文化因素扮演着最重要的角色之一。作为英语学习者,中国人如果未能了解目标语相关的文化因素,那么语用失误将不可避免。语言和文化密不可分这一话题已是老生常谈。因此,英语语言学习者不仅需要了解新语言的词汇和句法,而且还要学习外语语言中包含的社会规范。

在跨文化交际过程中,语用失误频繁出现,因此对其高度重视是很有必要的。Thomas 认为,语用失误产生于语用迁移。也就是说,在没有考虑到交际规则的情况下,拥有不同文化背景的人直接将他们各自的本土语言转换为目标语,而交际规则正是他们所要重视的。人类学家认为,人不仅是社会人,也是文化人。中国人在见面打招呼时喜欢询问对方的情况,以表示亲切和关怀。然而英国人更倾向于谈论天气来展开话题,这可以看出两国文化的差异性。如果在跨文化交际过程中忽视文化的差异性,那将会不可避免地导致语用迁移,继而产生语用失误。

Thomas 对语用失误的重要性做过评价。根据其观点,语法的错误使用可能会阻碍交流。一旦听话人意识到说话人的语法能力不强,母语使用者很可能对此怀有谅解的态度。但是语用失误则不然。如果非母语使用者说话看似流利,则母语使用者很可能不会将其明显的无礼归咎于语言能力的缺乏,而是归咎于粗鲁或敌意。

从理论上讲,语用失误可以避免。首先,应该将语言和文化差异性加以重视。文化是多元的、复杂的,而且无孔不入。语言是构成文化的主要组成部分之一,文化同时也能在很大程度上由语言反映出来。人们就是通过语言来描述周围环境以及与他人分享心情。在与他人交流的过程中,个人必须重视源语和目标语之间的文化差异。因为目标语相对于个体来说是一个全新的世界,许多陌生的因素会出现在他的文化领域中。因此,个体需要对目标语的文化进行了解,以便获得真正的语言能力,从而避免语用失误。其次,必须重视与一般语言能力不同的跨文化语用能力。根据 Chomsky 的观点,语言能力是指在理想情况下,母语使用者在其语言的使用中,能够从语法的层面,或是仅从语法的层面,对语句进行构建和辨析。这种能力并不足以使使用者有效地使用语言,而是用于有时候人们未能接受在语法层面使用的语言,或是非语法层面使用的语言得到认同这两种情况下。因此,除去语法层面,很显然还有一些其他的因素对语言能力有影响。鉴于此,Hymes 提出了"交际能力"的观点,这个观点是对 Chomsky 所提出的"语言能力"和"语法能力"的补充。在这之后,Widdowson 将此加以推进,提出"跨文化语用能力"的观点。这个观点包含两部分:在话语中识别上下文的能力;有能力理解在特殊话语中说话人有意传达的思想。培养和加强语用能力有利于在跨文化交际中减少语用失误。

中国的英语教学应该对外语教学策略做出反思和调整。何自然认为,随着英语学习者语法能力的加强,他们的语用能力不一定能自然而然地得到提升。在课堂教学中,外语的交流对话练习会跟随教师教给学生的语法结构进行,这一点教师或许拥有出色的表现。然而,真正的自然交流情景是不可预知的,绝非事先安排。如此一来,尽管学习者拥有坚实的语法基础和广泛的词汇量,但还是会有束缚,不能实现交际目的。

本研究旨在列举和分析跨文化交际过程中所导致语用失误的各种原因和因素,并给予中国英语学习者一些方法策略,从而避免语用失误。通过仔细且大量的研究发现,中国英语学习者跨文化语用能力的发展处于落后阶段,而且相比于语法能力的学习与培养,在很大程度上,跨文化语用能力被忽视。为了解决这个问题,本研究基于一些教育学原则的基础,对在外语学习和教学中如何培养语用能力,提出了一些建议。

本书由 6 章构成。第 1 章简要介绍了语用失误作为跨文化交际成功的障碍因素,强调对于语用失误研究和分析的重要性。

在第 2 章,笔者回顾了与语用学相关的跨文化交际研究领域的一些基本概念。语言、文化和交际是相互交织的系统。语言是文化组成的核心部分,文化主要通过语言反映出来。人们通过交际活动,学习文化、展示文化、传播文化,最终将文化保存下来。

交际能力、跨文化交际能力和语用能力是 Hymes 和 Widdowson 分别提出来的。如果外语学习者只强调语文能力或者语法能力,他们的语言和语法准确性自不必说。如果学习者将语用能力置于首位,那么他们将会关注在特殊语境中语言使用的"恰当性"问题,来确保交际目标的实现。此外,跨文化意识对减少语用失误是必不可少的。

在第 3 章,笔者回顾和分析了了和语用失误相关的主要语用学理论,包括 Austin 的言语行为理论,Searle 的间接言语行为理论,Grice 的合作原则,以及 Leech 的礼貌原则和中国学者顾曰国的礼貌原则。同时,笔者运用这些理论对一些语用失误的实例进行了分析,集中分析了语言交际过程中的语用差异问题,这些语用差异来源于文化多元性,对交际失误会产生直接的影响。

第 4 章是本研究的核心内容,主要探讨跨文化交际过程中的语用失误问题。笔者主要对两种类型的语用失误进行了探讨,一类是语言语用失误,另一类是社交语用失误。

第 5 章主要探讨为了减少和避免语用失误,必须采取一些措施和策略培养学习者的语用能力。在很大程度上,减少和避免语用失误与外语学习者的学习方法和教师的教学方法息息相关。因此,笔者提出了关于提升和改善学习者语用能力的一些措施和方法。

最后,笔者认为语用失误存在并贯穿于跨文化交际活动的始终。学习者的语言或语文能力与其相应的语用能力并不成正比。而本研究期望能达到以下目的:中国外语学习者和教师应该首先关注语用失误问题,在跨文化交际过程中顺利实现交际目标。

CHAPTER 2 ASPECTS OF INTERCUL-TURAL COMMUNICATION IN RELATION TO PRAGMATIC CONCERNS

Communicative competence, cross-cultural communicative competence and cross-cultural pragmatic competence are hierarchically related. Language, culture and communication are within a closely-knitted system where language is the core of culture, culture is reflected through language and transmitted, learned, kept and evolved through communication.

The three notions, communicative competence, cross-cultural communicative competence and cross-cultural pragmatic competence are proposed by Hymes and Widdowson. If foreign language learners focus on the linguistic competence and grammatical competence, they will certainly emphasize the grammatical accuracy and strictness. However, if their chief objective is to cultivate the pragmatic competence, they will pay attention to the "tactfulness" of language use in specific context so as to guarantee smooth process of communication. Therefore, learners' cross-cultural awareness is highly important in reducing pragmatic failures in communication.

2.1 Language, Culture and Communication

Language is the primary and most highly elaborated form of human symbolic activity. Language is human-specific. It is not a neutral medium that passes freely and easily into the private property of the speaker's intentions. It is populated, or overpopulated with the intention of others. According to Halliday, language is one of the semiotic systems that constitute a culture. Language meaning is directly related to our experience. It is the primary means by which a culture transits its beliefs, values, and norms. In light of the Sapir-Whorf hypothesis, language influences perceptions and transmits thoughts, and helps pattern them. Language is the principal means whereby we conduct our social lives. When it is used in contexts of communication, it is bound up with culture in multiple and complex ways. Language expresses cultural reality and symbolizes cultural reality as well.

According to Brown, culture is the contexts within which we exist, think, feel and relate to others. It is the "glue" that binds a group of people together. Larson and Smalley describe culture as a "blueprint" that guides the behavior of people in a community and is incubated in family life. It governs our behavior in groups, makes us sensitive to matters of status, and helps us know what others expect from us and what will happen if we do not live up to their expectations. Culture helps us to know how far we can go as individuals and what our responsibility is to the group.

Culture might be defined as the ideas, customs, skills, arts and tools, which characterize a given group of people in a given period. However, culture is more than the sum of its parts. "It is a system of integrated patterns, most of which remain below the threshold of consciousness, yet all of which govern human behavior just as surely as the manipulated strings of a puppet control its motions".

Culture is important to communication. Samovar states that culture is communication and communication is culture, and culture and communication are directly linked.

Culture has the strongest influence on the communication behavior. Many aspects of human communication are conditioned by culture: what topic is suitable in a conversation; how to respond to a message which is far from the home culture. The outcome of any communicative event is affected by how messages are conveyed, interpreted and reacted, which is culture-specific.

When members of different cultures join together to share ideas and information, then culture-loaded information may block the process of communicating in every state of the communication，namely，expressing，interpreting and reacting. Gumperz assumes that the actual communicative processes are first analyzed solely at the level of content and then interpreted in the extralinguistic cultural information. The understanding of the information relies both on linguistic presupposition and the culture-bound knowledge.

2.2　Intercultural Awareness and Pragmatic Concerns

As far as intercultural communication is concerned，cross-culture research has shown that there are indeed some characteristics of culture that make one culture different from another.

Cross-cultural or intercultural communication usually refers to the meeting of two cultures across the political boundaries of nations. It occurs whenever a message sender is a member of one culture and a message receiver is that of another culture. Intercultural communication may also refer to communication between people from different ethnic，social，gender cultures within the boundary of the same national language.

We may find intercultural communication difficult. Even if we overcome the natural barriers of language differences，we may fail to understand and to be understood. Misunderstanding may become the inherent problem in intercultural communication.

Intercultural awareness may be the most important element in the process of intercultural communication. The reason why the author enunciates intercultural awareness is that it has much effect on the extent of pragmatic failures. It is one thing to have some knowledge of world conditions. It is another thing to comprehend and accept the consequences of the basic human capacity for creating unique cultures—with the resultant profound differences in outlook and practice manifested among societies. Attainment of intercultural awareness at a high level will require methods that counter those resisting forces which stand in the way of intercultural communication. According to Hanvey，four levels of intercultural awareness are discriminated. At the first level，awareness of superficial or very visible cultural traits is attained through textbooks, magazines. At the second level, it is the awareness of significant and subtle cultural traits that contrast markedly with one's own through culture conflict situations. At the third level, awareness of significant and subtle cultural traits that contrast markedly with one's own is reached by intellectual analysis. The fourth level is the awareness of how another culture feels from the standpoint of the insider by immersing in that culture.

From the four levels of intercultural awareness, we may conclude that the first two levels involve the contact with the surface of certain culture; whereas the last two levels involve the deep structure of certain culture. That means getting inside the head of the strangers and looking out at the world through their eyes. It involves cognitive matters.

Byram believed that culture is contained in both the pragmatics and semantics of language. Pragmatics deals with the effect that language has on human perceptions and behaviors. A pragmatic analysis of language goes beyond phonology, morphology, semantics, and syntax. Instead, it considers how users of a particular language are able to understand the meaning of specific utterances in particular contexts, For example, when you are eating a meal with a group of people and somebody says, "Is there any tea?" You know that you should give the person a cup of tea rather than simply answer "yes".

The pragmatics of language use can affect intercultural communication. Imagine an American is a dinner guest in a Chinese household. He has just eaten adelicious meal. He is relatively full but not so full that it will be impossible for him to eat more if it is considered socially appropriate to do so. Consider the following dialogue:

HOSTESS: I see that your plate is empty. Would you like some more Jiaozi?

American: No, thank you. It was delicious, but I'm quite full.

HOSTESS: Please, you must have some more to eat.

American: No, thank you. I've really had enough.

HOSTESS: Are you sure that you won't have any more? You really seemed to enjoy Jiaozi.

From this conversation, we can see that the embarrassing situation indeed takes place when the two speakers misunderstand each other. As for the hostess, the diner's negative response is not interpreted as a true negative response in light of the Chinese culture. As for the diner, the hostess is over-hospitable, or showing too much concern for his privacy. Because of the lack of pragmatic knowledge, the two speakers haven't achieved the desired results in communication. Even if a person knows the target language, he has to know the pragmatics of language use lest he should be stuck in the conflict of intercultural communication.

2.3　Communicative Competence, Intercultural Communicative Competence and Pragmatic Competence

Since cultural differences create dissimilar meaning and expectations that require even greater levels of communication skill, communicative competence is an even more difficult objective to achieve. When it comes to the concept of "competence", we may think of Chomsky's definition of "competence" as "the speaker-hearer's knowledge of his language". Competence is an idealization. It is the knowledge of the "ideal speaker-listener operating within a homogeneous speech community".

Hymes argues that the concept of competence by Chomsky simply means knowledge of the language system, or grammatical knowledge. It is called linguistic competence. If the speakers and hearers are far from ideal and their language behavior cannot be characterized as that of any "homogeneous speech community", then we have to accept that this involves far more than the knowledge of grammar. If a speaker were to produce grammatical sentences without regard to the situations in which they were being used, he would certainly be considered mental disorder.

In contrast to linguistic competence, which centers on one's grammatical knowledge, Hymes puts forward the idea of communicative competence. He lists four sectors. The first sector is whether or not something is formally possible. It is concerned with whether a sentence is grammatical or ungrammatical. The second sector is whether something is psychologically acceptable. The third sector is whether something is appropriate in relation to a context in which it is used and evaluated. A sentence can be grammatically possible, feasible, but inappropriate. The last sector concerns the ability to judge whether something is done.

After careful study on the communicative competence, Canale and Swain conclude that communicative competence is composed of four aspects: grammatical competence; sociolinguistic competence; linguistic strategic competence; discourse competence. The last three aspects may be considered pragmatic competence.

As far as intercultural communicative competence is concerned, Gudykunst (1984) maintains that intercultural communicative competence includes cognitive competence, affective competence and behavioral competence. Furthermore, pragmatic competence and episodic competence are also included. Cognitive competence, affective competence and behavioral competence are affiliated to man's adaptive ability. These belong to a man's psychological scope, which needs adjusting all the time. Here, what we are much more concerned with is pragmatic competence and episodic competence, particularly the former. Pragmatic competence refers to fact that how interactors communicate flexibly on the premise of their mastery of communicative language. It includes such principles as the cooperative principle, the politeness principle through interpersonal interaction, and the principle of discourse organization and turn-taking.

In sum, pragmatic competence is an indispensable and primary sector of intercultural competence. A man's index of pragmatic competence determines whether the process of intercultural communication goes well or not. If pragmatic competence is taken as the chief objective, then the target of communication can be achieved, thus pragmatic failures may be avoided.

第2章　语用学中的跨文化交际

交际能力、跨文化交际能力和跨文化语用能力这三个概念是层层递进,密不可分的。语言、文化和交流三者组成了相互交织的系统。语言在文化成分中视为普遍之核心,文化通过语言得以大量反映。通过交流,文化得以学习、演绎、传播和保存。

交际能力、跨文化交际能力和语用能力这三个概念是由 Hymes 和 Widdowson 二人提出。如果外语学习者专注于语言能力和语法能力,他们一定会特别重视语言的语法严谨性。如果他们的主要目标是培养语用能力,那么为了保证交流的正常进行,学习者将重视在特定情形下语言的"得体性"。可见,学习者跨文化意识在减少其语用失误中十分重要。

2.1　语言、文化与交际

语言是人类活动中最主要和最精致的代表形式,为人类所特有。语言并非是中性介质,能够自由且轻易地变成说话者意向的私有财产。语言是多元化的,又或是随着其他意向的增加而出现过剩。根据 Halliday 所言,语言是构成文化的一种符号系统。语言意义与我们的生活经验息息相关,它是信仰、价值观以及规则的主要传播途径。根据 Sapir - Whorf 假说所述,语言可以影响人的认知,传播思想,并且有助于将其组合形成模板范式。人们的社交活动主要凭借语言这一主要途径进行。语言在实际交流的过程中,与各种文化会产生千丝万缕的联系。语言能够反映且代表文化现实。

Brown 曾指出,人们在文化的大背景下生存、思考、感受,并且与他人发生联系。文化是人们聚集在一起的"黏合剂"。Larson 和 Smalley 将文化描述为能够在团体中指导人们行为的"蓝图",认为文化由家庭生活培养而成。人们在群体中的行为由文化指导,文化使人们对身份地位富有敏感性,帮助人们了解他人对自己的期待,以及辜负他人期许的后果。文化帮助人们了解每个人的发展路径,以及在群体生活中所承担的责任。

文化或许会被当作在特定时期中,特定人群中的各种理念、习俗、技能、艺术或工具。然而,文化并不单单是其各种特色的集合。文化是一种综合模式系统,其中大部分未超过意识层面,但其全部整体却能够指导人们的行为,这正如同操控提线木偶一样。

文化在交流过程中十分重要。文化既是交流,交流也是文化。文化和交流相互联系,不可分割。

文化对沟通行为的影响巨大。人们在交流过程中的诸多方面受到文化的制约:在交流中应该选择什么话题;如何回应与自身文化大相径庭的信息。任何交际事件的结果都受到了信息传递、解读和相互作用的影响,人们将此称为文化特异性。

当各种文化聚集在一起分享理念和信息时,文化负载信息可能会阻碍交流过程中的各个环节,即表达、解读和相互间的反应。Gumperz 认为,实际中的交流过程首先会单独从内容层面进行分析,接着会从语言之外的文化层面进行解读。对信息的理解依赖于语言预设和文化知识。

2.2　跨文化意识与语用观

就关注跨文化交际而言,跨文化研究表明了在文化中的确包含着一些特性使其与其他文化出现差异。

跨文化或跨文化交际通常是指国家间跨行政边界的两种文化之间的交流,发生在信息发出者和信息接收者之间,两者拥有不同的文化背景。跨文化交际也可以指拥有不同民族、社会地位、性别文化的人们,在使用相同语言国度环境中的交际活动。

人们会发现跨文化交际并非易事。即使跨越了不同语言之间的天然屏障,但人们还是无法做到对他人了解,或让他人了解自己。在跨文化交际中,误解与生俱来,不可避免。

跨文化意识或许是在跨文化交际过程中最重要的因素,这是因为其在语用失误中的影响巨大。一方面,它能使人们对世界产生一定的认识;另一方面,了解和接受由人们所拥有的基本能力而创造出来的独特文化,这种文化拥有深层次的积淀,在社会生活中可展现不同的前景和实用性。对于高层次跨文化意识的获取,应该立足于阻碍跨文化交际因素的对立面。根据 Hanvey 所述,应该通过四个层面对跨文化意识进行辨析。在第一层面中,人们通过教科书、杂志等渠道获取一些明显易得的文化特质意识。在第二层面中,一些显著且细微的文化特质意识与各种情形下的个人所有文化产生的鲜明对比。在第三层面中,一些显著且细微的文化特质意识与个人通过智能分析所产生的文化形成鲜明对比。在第四层面中,通过沉浸在一种文化中,从其内部人的角度,看待另一种文化的感受。

从上述跨文化意识的四个层面可知,前两个层面是指某种文化的表层联系,而后两种是指某种文化的深层次结构。这就意味着要进入陌生人的想法之中,并且用他们的视角看待世界,这种做法就包含了认知的过程和内容。

Byram 认为,文化在语用学和语义学中都有体现。语用学研究的是语言对人们认知和行为的影响。语言的语用分析超出了音位学、构词学、语义学和句法学的范围。然而,它却研究了特定语言使用者如何理解在特定环境背景下的特定话语。例如,当你和一群人共同进餐时,其中有人说:"有茶么?",你知道应该给那个人一杯茶,而非简单地回答"有"。

语言中的语用学会对跨文化交际产生影响。我们可以构建一个画面,一位美国人在中国家庭中做客。他刚刚吃饱一顿大餐,但相对并未吃撑。如果因为社交需要,他还是能够再吃一些的。所以,参考以下对话:

HOSTESS：I see that your plate is empty. Would you like some more Jiaozi?

American：No, thank you. It was delicious，but I'm quite full.

HOSTESS：Please, you must have some more to eat.

American：No, thank you. I've really had enough.

HOSTESS：Are you sure that you won't have any more? You really seemed to enjoy Jiaozi.

从上述对话中,我们可以看出,当双方之间出现误解后,会造成尴尬的局面。在中国文化中,对于女主人来说,她并没有将客人的否定回答当作真正的否定意义。从客人的角度出发来看,女主人过于热情,而且显得对自己的隐私过于关注。正是因为缺乏语用知识,双方才未能达到原本的交流目的。即使一个人了解目标语,此人也需要懂得使用语言的语用规范,否则就会陷入跨文化交际的矛盾中。

2.3　交际能力、跨文化交际能力与语用能力

因为文化差异导致了语言意义和期望的不同,这就需要更高级别的交际技巧,所以获得交际能力就显得更加困难。在讨论"能力"这一概念时,我们应该考虑到 Chomsky 将"能力"定义为"说话者-听话者驾驭其自身语言的能力"。这里的能力是理想化的。这种能力指的是"在理想化层面,说话人-听话人在同种言语社区中使用语言"。

Hymes 认为 Chomsky 所提出能力的概念仅仅表明了语言系统知识或语法知识,将其称为语言能力。如果说话人和听话人并非在理想层面且他们之间的语言行为没有任何"同种言语社区"关联。那么,我们就应该认识到这与语法知识的关联度相距甚远。如果说话人的话语中拥有语法支撑,但并没有考虑到话语使用的情景,那此人一定会被看作是精神失常的表现。

相比于注重一个人语法知识的语言能力来说,Hymes 提出了交际能力的理念。他将其分为四个部分。第一部分是就表达形式上的合理与否进行的探讨,其关注点在句子是否合乎语法。第二部分关注的是能否从心理学角度得以接受。第三部分关注点在于,在已使用或评估后的上下文背景下的合理性,即一句话在语法层面合理可行,但并不恰当。最后一部分关注的是对交际者的表达能力问题。

在对交际能力仔细研究后,Canale 和 Swain 认为交际能力由四部分组成:语法能力;社会语言能力;语言技巧能力;语篇能力。后三种可以认定为语用能力。

对于跨文化交际能力而言,Gudykunst 认为此项能力包含认知能力、情感能力和行为能力,此外还包含了语用能力和情节能力。认知能力、情感能力和行为能力与人的适应力不可分割,属于心理学范畴,需要随时对其做出调整。因此,对于语用能力和情节能力来讲,我们更加关注前者。语用能力指的是在交际语言的精湛运用中,交流者们如何更加灵活地进行交谈。这就包含了一些交际原则,如合作原则、人际交互中的礼貌原则、话语组织和话题交互的原则。

总而言之,语用能力在跨文化能力中不可或缺,而且占据主要地位。一个人的语用能力大小决定了跨文化交际是否能够顺利进行。如果将语用能力看作首要目标,那么才能达到交流的目的,从而避免语用失误。

CHAPTER 3   THEORETICAL PER-SPECTIVES ON PRAGMATIC FAILURES

As far as the effectireness and affainment of interculfural communiation are comcerned, communicators' interculfural competence and pragmatic competerce play important roles. In addition pragmatic factors, including the oretical and practical ones, should also be considered so as to achiere smooth communication.

3.1   Pragmatic Theoretical Considerations

Before we probe into the center of pragmatic failure, we had better take an overall look at the pragmatic perspective. According to Verschueren, pragmatics is defined as a general cognitive, social, and cultural perspective on linguistic phenomena in relation to their usage in forms of behavior. Some other linguists define it as the study of those relations between language and context that are grammaticalized, or encoded in the structure of a language. He Ziran puts it as follows: Pragmatics studies the specific utterance in specific situation. It studies how to understand and make use of language through context.

In the process of intercultural communication, the understanding of pragmatic principles is much relevant to the correctness and appropriateness of language use, and to the reduction of pragmatic failures as well. Since pragmatic principles are characterized by generality and social, cultural relativity, we may look into the pragmatic failures by applying some ideas in pragmatic theories.

3.1.1 Deictic Features

The single most obvious way in which the relationship between language and context is reflected in the structure of languages themselves is through the level of deixis. Essentially deixis is mainly used to signify the participant in the talk, the space in which the talk occurs, the time and social setting where the talk takes place. The specific deictic expressions are context-dependent. The importance of deictic information for the interpretation of utterances is perhaps best illustrated by what happens when such information is lacking. Let's consider the following sentence.

(1)I'll be back in half an hour. If we interpret the sentence in isolation, or without referring to any context, we may see it conveys no information. Because we don't know when it was written, we cannot know when the writer will return. Or, imagine that the lights go out as Harry has just begun saying.

(2)Listen, I'm not disagreeing with *you* but with *you*, and not about *this* but about *this*. We don't know you refer to whom and whom; and this indicates what without the contextual knowledge. All these expressions depend, for their interpretation, on the speaker and hearer's sharing the same context. If a person speaks to you I'll arrive tomorrow morning face to face, you will have no doubt about his arrival. But if a careless person sends you a telegram from the opposite side of the earth, it reads arrive 11:00 am tomorrow, you must think hard to know when he will arrive actually. The trouble lies in the time-difference. People in China and people in USA have different ideas concerning the exact time tomorrow and 11:00 am. So, we must have a clear point of reference to understand the deictic items. In language communication, this point of reference is located with the speakers. The person in the center of communication is just the person who is speaking. Therefore it is clear that the time the speaker is speaking is the deictic center; the place where the speaker is speaking is the central place. Thus, the deictic items in language are organized on the basis of speakers.

The above statements we have mentioned are mainly about the deictic use. That is, the referent of the deixis and its implication shift with the changing of context. The traditional categories of deixis are person, place and time. Instudying person deixis, we notice that "I am in the last place" is often used to indicate that the speaker is in the last place. But this sentence is also used on a number of occasions to indicate that somebody else is in the last place. For example, you are watching a race and the person upon whom you have bet, No.2, drops to the last place. "I am in the last place!" You exclaim in anger to your companion. Your companion knows perfectly well what you mean—that the person upon whom you have bet is in the last place. Indeed, she replies in kind, disagreeing with your statement. "No, you aren't. Look, you are passing No. 3!" The success of such communication must be built on a certain context; otherwise misunderstanding may arise.

Some motion verbs that have built-in deictic components are worth considering. In English, "come" and "go" make some sort of distinction between the directions of motion relative to participants in the speech event. We may note that "He is coming" seems to gloss as "he is moving towards the speaker's location" while "He is going" glosses as "He is moving away from the speaker's location" in terms of Chinese understanding. In light of this explanation, "I'm coming to London" seems illogical. But In English, there is a habitual use: when the destination of the speaker's motion is equivalent to the hearer's location, the deictic center is on the hearer rather than on the speaker. This is perhaps a kind of politeness. Therefore, "come" is used when the movement goes towards the location of the hearer. In practice, let's suppose a Chinese student makes an appointment with his or her classmate to pay a visit. In this case, we should say "Can I come to your home tomorrow?" instead of "Can I go to your home tomorrow?"

In terms of time deixis, we notice that such deictic words as "yesterday" "today" and "tomorrow" preempt the calendrical or absolute ways of referring to the relevant days. Interestingly, native English speakers always tend to use them. The pre-emptive rule goes as follows: In referring to the same time, we tend to use the more general, uncertain time deixis rather than those absolute time deixis. Let's compare the following sentences.

(1)I'm going to leave here on Thursday.

(2)I'm going to leave here today.

(3) I'm going to leave here tomorrow.

If "today" is Thursday, English people are liable to use sentence (2). If "today" is Wednesday, they'd rather use sentence (3) than use sentence (1). If we still use sentence (1), then "Thursday" can only be referred to next Thursday (or perhaps some more remote Thursday). Sometimes English and Chinese people are not in agreement with the expression of time deixis. If an Englishman says "It will be held next Thursday", then next Thursday equals Chinese "下周的星期四" on the condition that the present speaking time is from Wednesday to Sunday. If the time is Monday or Tuesday, then an ambiguity arises. Next Thursday can either refer to the Thursday of this week or that Thursday after nine or ten days.

What are reflected in the above statements show that the interpretation of deictic expressions depends on the context and the speaker's intention. Deictic expressions always convey much more than what is said. Deixis appears to be a universal feature of human communication. From an intercultural point of view, we may be aware that deictic expressions are sometimes culture-specific. In studying the pragmatic failures, we suggest that more weight be put on this aspect.

3.1.2　Speech Acts Considerations

Of all the issues in the general theory of language usage, speech acts theory has probably aroused the widest interest. This theory studies the communicative functions that one word or one sentence produces in specific contexts.

In attempting to express themselves, people not only produce utterances containing grammatical structures and words, they perform actions through those utterances. Actions performed via utterances are generally called speech acts. Speech acts are commonly given more specific labels, such as apology, complaint, compliment, invitation, promise or request. These speech acts apply to the speaker's communicative intention in producing an utterance.

On any occasion, the action performed by producing an utterance consists of three related acts. Austin isolates three basic senses in which in saying something one is doing something, and hence three kinds of acts are simultaneously performed:

(1)Locutionary act: the utterance of a sentence with determinate sense and reference.

(2)Illocutionary act: the making of a statement, offer, promise, etc. in uttering a sentence, by virtue of the conventional force associated with it (or with its explicit performative paraphrase).

(3)Perlocutionary act : the bringing about of effects being special to the circumstances of utterance.

The nucleus of Austin's statement is "saying is believing". In the process of intercultural communication, more often than not, the illocutionary act and perlocutionary act are the focus of our interest. Sometimes the speaker's illocutionary act cannot be understood very well or effectively by the audience. Therefore, some kinds of polysemy or ambiguity may be formed. As a result, the perlocutionary act can't be achieved satisfactorily so that the expressive intention of the speaker's speech act contradicts with its effect. So it is necessary for us to contrast and analyze the differences in people's operational process of speech acts and the corresponding pragmatic failures in terms of various cultural backgrounds.

(4) In a discussion of English class, the English teacher Mr X told his students that his wife Mrs X would not go to the class and join with them in the discussion, and he felt very sorry for this. Later on, one Chinese student talked about himself and said: "Like Mrs X, I've also caught a very bad cold, yet I have to come to class." At this point Mr X chipped in before the student finished his remark: "But you have a very tough constitution."

It can be seen clearly that Mr X's remark is explanatory and compelled. His student's statement has a negative effect on Mr X's thought, emotion or act. That is a kind of perlocutionary act, which makes Mr X embarrassed. On the student's side, he simply focuses on his statement that he has to attend the class even if he has got the bad cold as Mrs X. The student's statement results in a kind of illocutionary force. As for Mr X, the student associates himself with Mrs X and wonders why Mrs X didn't attend the class like him. Consequently, it is not hard to understand why Mr X defends himself so impatiently.

(5) In a translation class, the teacher, Mr X is inspecting the assignment he gave to the students the other day. He asks the students to read out their revised versions for further discussion.

Mr X: Miss A, did you revise your own version?

Miss A:No, I didn't. I still stick to my original version. I think it is too soon to do it.

Mr X:You think your original version is perfect.

Miss A: ...

In this conversation, Mr X intends to get Miss A to read her revised version. This speech act is based on his assumption that students are responsible for the fulfillment of the assignment. When he speaks,"Did you revise your own version?" he doesn't inquire whether his student has finished the assignment or not. What he intends to stress in his locutionary act is just to give out a mild command. Unfortunately, Miss A misunderstands his request. She just takes it for granted that the illocutionary act of Mr X's utterance is to check her homework. Of course her reply is rejected by Mr X. Although Miss A doesn't contradict Mr X on purpose, yet the pragmatic failure takes place. The key point is that Miss A mistakes the illocutionary force of Mr X's utterance. Under this circumstance, the perlocutionary act of Mr X's utterance produces such an effect that Miss A feels so tense that she has to defend herself immediately. If she understands well the communicative function and pragmatic meaning of the speech acts, then some failure or awkward deadlock may be avoided to some extent. In a sense, Miss A's response could be improved as "Perhaps in a day or two when I look at it again, I'll change my mind."

(6) On a train, a Chinese hits his head against the window as the train stops. Seeing this, an American sitting next to him expresses his pity.

American:I am sorry.

Chinese:It's not your fault.

Here, some pragmatic failure occurs in the communication. When the

American says, "I am sorry", the effect of the illocutionary force is just to show sympathy for the Chinese. But the Chinese misunderstands the expression of sympathy for an apology. It is no wonder the American is puzzled about the reply.

Searle holds that speech acts have the function in carrying out multiple dimensions of meaning of utterance in different social and cultural settings, whereas the specific and particular social conventions and cultural norms will be the key points in deciding the accurate information which the speaker conveys and the hearer receives. In many cases, cross-cultural communicative activities come to a deadlock owing to the different cultural background.

Greetings play a very important role in interpersonal communication. It is the beginning of communication. If they are not used properly, most probably the communicative process may be interrupted. We Chinese usually greet each other in this way: "你出去啊?" or "你上哪儿去?" In the Chinese culture, the illocutionary force and the effect of them is just the exchange of conventional greetings. But if we say "Where are you going?" to an American, the original illocutionary force will be lost, the illocutionary act will not be sensed. On the contrary, the American will take it for granted that the illocutionary force of "Where are you going?" is that you want to inquire about his or her privacy. Under such circumstances, the expected perlocutionary act will not take place for certain. At this moment, the communicative activity will come to an end.

In different cultural settings, the expressions of refuse or rejection reflect the connotations of different cultures. Refusing somebody or rejecting someone implies some degree of impoliteness or rudeness in light of the Chinese cultural tradition. In other words, the speech acts of the Chinese people are restricted by "the politeness principle" and maintained by "face work". In refusing others, the Chinese people usually try to express tactfully and indirectly lest they hurt other people's "face". But in the Western culture, this concept of "saving face" doesn't exist. Many English people are liable to be puzzled about "losing face" proposed by Chinese. An American businessman was in negotiation with his Chinese counterpart over some important sectors of investment. After that, he wanted to know whether his project was accepted or not. Then the Chinese just repeated the Chinese type wording "We'll think this over again." or "We must give it more thought." In fact, what the Chinese meant to express is "No, we don't agree with your proposal." But the American didn't realize the effect of illocutionary force, which suggested "disagree". He took it for granted that the other party would reconsider it sooner or later. So the American waited for the reply and the result was self-evident. The effect of the perlocutionary act was against the Chinese expectation. We discover from this case that the expression of refusal in the English culture is more straightforward and direct. By contrast, the expression of refusal in Chinese is more indirect and the "meaning" of a locutionary act is not in accordance with the "force" of an illocutionary act, and sometimes they are quite different.

In terms of speech acts of compliments, the illocutionary acts of some compliments can be regarded as the implication of some other intentions. For instance, when an Englishman expresses appreciation for a Chinese lady "You are attractive", the illocutionary act serves as the function of praise, and the perlocutionary act is intended to make her pleased and happy. But the response of this Chinese lady is characterized by blushing with embarrassment. For in China, the compliment to a woman's beauty by an unfamiliar man may be considered as an unsuitable and frivolous conduct. The act of complimenting a woman's appearance is most possibly taken as a taboo by the Chinese people. Therefore, such complimenting utterance doesn't bring an intended result, but rather make her embarrassed against the background of Chinese culture.

3.1.3 Indirect Speech Acts Considerations

According to Searle, under most circumstances the speech act is performed indirectly through the performance of another speech act. He points out that usually speakers perform on illocutionary act implicitly by way of performing another illocutionary act explicitly. The explicitly performed act is used to convey another speech act; and the speaker relies on background knowledge and mental capacities that he shares with the hearer in order to achieve understanding.

For most indirect speech acts, there must be inferent-triggers, i. e., some indications that the literal meanings or literal forces are conversationally inadequate in the context and must be "repaired" by some inference. Look at the following dialogue.

(1) A: Let's go to the movie tonight.

B: I have to study for the exam.

B's reply conveys such information: I'm afraid I can't go with you tonight. As a result, it is likely that A is willing to accept this refusal. But if the two sides do not share the common knowledge or common background, the unexpressed information which B's utterance carries would not be understood by A. Sometimes, the listener's understanding toward an indirect speech act by the speaker may not be in agreement with the intention of its illocutionary act on account of the lack of mutual knowledge.

(2) Aunt: Won't you have another piece of cake, Tommy?

Tommy: No, I thank you.

Aunt: You seem to be suffering from loss of appetite.

Tommy: That isn't loss of appetite. What I'm suffering from is politeness.

When Tommy replies "No, I thank you", some kind of indirect illocutionary intention lies in it. Tommy and Aunt lack a certain degree of common knowledge. Aunt merely understands the literal meaning of Tommy's refusal. She doesn't understand the indirect illocutionary intention in Tommy's "No, I thank you". What Tommy really intends to express is that he is ready to accept the offer of cakes by his Aunt. He doesn't express his idea directly because he feels a little bit strange or unfamiliar before his Aunt. This example shows that it is not proper to make indirect speech act at a certain time or in a certain place if the speaker and hearer lack some contextual conditions or background information.

In our daily life, when a person pays a visit to his friend or colleague, the following conversation often takes place in a Chinese family.

(3) Host: It's getting dark. I suppose you haven't had your supper yet. Stay with us and have a dinner.

Guest：It doesn't matter. I have already finished.

In this talk，the illocutionary act of the host's utterance doesn't reflect the host's care for the guest. Rather，it implies "It's high time you came back." Unfortunately，the guest doesn't get the host's illocutionary point. Consequently，the guest's reply to the host's utterance sounds inappropriate.

（4）A tourist guide led a group of English people to the coach. The driver didn't turn on the air-conditioner，so it is very hot and sultry inside the coach. One tourist said：

Tourist：Oh，it reminds me of my Vesuvius tour（威苏威火山之旅）last summer.

Guide：Oh，you've traveled a lot.

In fact，the illocutionary force of the tourist's utterance implies some kind of dissatisfaction and request，that is，"It is too hot here. Is it possible that the driver turns on the air-conditioner a bit earlier?" But the tourist merely understands the literal meaning，thus causing misunderstanding.

3.1.4　The Cooperative Principle Considerations

Grice's concept of implicature is essentially a theory about how people use language. He holds that people involved in a conversation will cooperate with each other. Grice identifies four basic maxims of conversation underlying the efficient cooperative use of language，which jointly express a general cooperative principle. They are expressed as follows.

（1）The cooperative principle：Make your conversational contribution such as is required，at the stage at which it occurs，by the accepted purpose or direction of the talk exchange in which you are engaged.

（2）The maxim of Quality：try to make your contribution one that is true，specifically：

a. Do not say what you believe to be false.

b. Do not say that for which you lack adequate evidence.

（3）The maxim of Quantity：

a. Make your contribution as informative as is required for the current purposes of the exchange.

b. Do not make your contribution more informative than is required.

(4)The maxim of Relevance：

a. Make your contributions relevant.

(5)The maxim of Manner：Be perspicuous，and specifically：

a. Avoid obscurity.

b. Avoid ambiguity.

c. Be brief.

d. Be orderly.

In brief，what these maxims suggest is that people should speak sincerely，relevantly and clearly while providing sufficient information. Otherwise，communication will not go smoothly.

(6)A. Can you tell me how to make egg soup?

B. I have a recipe that got from my aunt.

A. (Puzzled) You didn't answer my question.

Here，the reason why A feels puzzled is that he doesn't consider the implicature of B's utterance in terms of the maxim of relevance. Yet B makes use of this maxim in his reply，meaning "I could offer you my aunt's recipe." Since A doesn't observe the cooperative principle，communication failure occurs.

The process of intercultural communication may be effective provided that the interactors observe these maxims；but on the other hand，these maxims may not be scaled equally by the interactors owing to their different cultures. A foreign teacher inquires if he is allowed to visit a Chinese teacher's class. The dean has a dialogue with him：

(7) Foreign teacher：I'd like to visit Miss Ma's class. Will that be all right?

Dean：I'm sure you understand our problems. Because of certain reasons，it may not be possible.

Here the dean's indirect reply to the foreign teacher's request violates the maxim of quantity，which produces conversational implicature. It makes the inquirer feel more puzzled about the feasibility and appropriateness of his request. In the Chinese culture，much information is decoded by the way of perceiving instead of by words，which is typical of the English culture. To avoid ambiguity and misunderstanding, the dean's reply should be a little more direct and straightforward, which is adaptable to the English way. So it is much better to say, "I'll have to tell Miss Ma but I doubt it."

In the Chinese-speaking context, social distance and social relationship are relatively steady, speakers of lower social status are dependent on those of higher status and are also obedient to them. In this case, they are quite different from Westerners in their adherence to the four maxims. Relatively speaking, Chinese speakers seem to attach more importance to the maxim of "manner" at the cost of the maxim of "quality" or "quantity". Usually, when the Chinese people are invited to dinner, and urged to eat something, they have the habit of saying "No, it is no need." In the Chinese culture, this may be understood as "Yes, please offer me again." But to the Americans, this is obviously a sign of refusal. Instead of saying "no" in refusing a request, the Chinese prefer to use ambiguous utterances. For example, "我们研究研究。"(we'll discuss it), "可能不方便吧!"(May be it will not be convenient) and so on. These responses seem ambiguous and thus are against Grice's maxim of quality, quantity and relevance but sound polite and natural to the native speakers of Chinese. As for the native speakers of English, they generally feel extremely frustrated and provocative at what they see as evasive replies to straightforward request.

3.2　Intercultural Pragmatic Contrastive Analysis

It is true that pragmatic failures originate from the cultural differences. In fact, people from different cultural backgrounds have different understandings towards some theories and rules connected with conversation and communication. Consequently, many failures and errors occur. In this sense, it is necessary for us to make a comparative study on such theories and principles in intercultural communication.

3.2.1　Politeness Principles in Chinese and English Culture

Because of different cultural backgrounds and values, Chinese and Westerners have different maxims of politeness. Here two politeness theories are to be introduced and contrasted. One is set up by Geoffrey Leech, who bases his theory chiefly on the language of English-speaking society; the other, by Gu Yueguo, has the features of Chinese society.

Leech specifies the basic maxims of politeness principle as follows:

(1) Tact Maxim (in impossitives and commissives).

a. Minimize cost to other.

b. Maximize benefit to other.

(2) Generosity Maxim (in impossitives and commissives).

a. Minimize benefit to self.

b. Maximize cost to self.

(3) Approbation Maxim (in expressives and assertives).

a. Minimize dispraise of other.

b. Maximize praise of other.

(4) Modesty Maxim (in expressives and assertives).

a. Minimize praise of self.

b. Maximize dispraise of self.

(5) Agreement Maxim (in assertives).

a. Minimize disagreement between self and other.

b. Maximize agreement between self and other.

(6) Sympathy Maxim (in assertives).

a. Minimize antipathy between self and other.

b. Maximize sympathy between self and other.

In real daily life, however, there are vastly different understandings between the Chinese and the English people. A polite behavior in the Chinese culture may be impolite in the English culture and vice versa. Take Tact and Generosity Maxims as an example. A Chinese host would insist on offering a cup of tea to an American guest by saying "Have a cup of tea" and would move to make it at once. Even if the guest does not want it at all and refuses it, the host would offer it several times and may even say something like "You must have a taste." or "You must drink some." When offering food, the Chinese would do the same to show his warmth and sincere involvement in offering, which might make the guest quite unhappy. The Chinese thinks he is maximizing benefit to the guest and maximizing cost to himself through inviting him for a drink and something to eat. He does not realize that his warmth and generosity have dominated the guest's individual right, freedom, and independence by his impositions. The more generous and warmer he is in this way, the unhappier the guest is.

In contrast to the politeness principle by Leech, Gu Yueguo concludes that the features of Chinese principle of politeness are respectfulness, modesty, attitudinal warmth and refinement. And he sets up five maxims.

(1) Dispraise of self and praise of other: dispraise self and anything relating to self; praise other and anything relating to other.

(2) Address: address each other according to the traditional ordered hierarchy to show the interpersonal relationship in the communication.

(3) Refinement: use refined words, with more indirectness and less directness.

(4) Agreement: maximize agreement between self and other.

(5) Good, word and deed: minimize cost and maximize benefit to other; maximize the benefit that self gets from other, and minimize the cost that self plays.

Influenced by the cultural backgrounds and values, politeness principles cannot be without the stamp of their cultures. In the following I will analyze some pragmatic failures in relevance to the politeness principles in the course ofintercultural communication.

(1) A Chinese, with his American friend, are dining at a restaurant.

American: I enjoy the meal very much.

Chinese: Taste this, eat slowly, eat more.

The Chinese behavior is tact and generous and it is very polite in the Chinese culture. But the same behavior is not proper in the English culture. Even if it maximizes benefit to the other, it offends the other's independence and freedom. How much one eats is his self-choice. And also, it is not decent to eat too much at a time, so the Chinese should say, "Help yourself, please." Otherwise, the American would find the Chinese impositive and domineering.

(2) An American manager praises his employee.

American manager: You have done a wonderful job.

Chinese employee: No, no. I didn't do it very well.

Modesty is one of the outstanding characteristics of the Chinese culture while in the American culture people do not value it that way. Chinese modesty is to put down self and to build up others whereas "modesty" in the politeness principle by Leech is avoiding self-praise. Chinese modesty is the core of Chinese politeness while the "Modesty Maxim" is not so important as the other maxims of Leech's politeness principle. Chinese modesty is a virtue of self-cultivation that is the foundation on which politeness is built whereas English modesty is a strategy of minimizing praise of self. That's why it tends to be hard for native speakers of English to understand many negative comments in Chinese which are expressed out of modesty.

An American professor, after finishing the lecture, conversed with a Chinese teacher. The Chinese teacher said to him, "You look rather tired. You had better take a good rest." In communication, Chinese would think more of others than self. But sometimes the Chinese tend to misuse sympathy maxim. Sympathy maxim means sharing what others feel. To show sympathy is to avoid antipathy. Not knowing how to avoid antipathy may cause serious communication failures between the Chinese and the English. Chinese people are more considerate of others in communication. They think that any considerate talk is polite. In this conversation, the Chinese teacher speaks out of his respect and concern for the foreign professor. This agrees with the sympathy maxim in the Chinese culture. But in the English culture, the foreign professor may consider the Chinese teacher is not satisfied with his lecture and implies some criticism in speaking so. It has far exceeded the American's understanding of concern or sympathy and it is very impolite in their culture.

What's more, in both Chinese and English culture, the tact maxim is presented and it is often interpreted in different approaches by the people of two cultures. An American invites a Chinese by saying, "Would you join us for dinner tonight?" the Chinese replies "No, thanks. It would be too much trouble for you." This reply is not within the American's expectation. Both the Chinese and the American observe their own "Tact maxim". The American thinks that he is minimizing cost and maximizing benefit to the

Chinese by inviting him to dinner, and that the reply by the Chinese is violating the tact maxim because refusing invitations without giving sound excuses is impolite in the American culture. As for the Chinese, however, he may think he is minimizing cost and trouble to the American and it is a polite convention in the Chinese culture to refuse other's offer several times before final acceptance.

3.3　Pragmatic Differences in Language Communication

Although the pragmatic conditions of communicative tasks are theoretically taken to be universal, the realizations of these tasks as social practices are culturally variable. Language communication is a process in which language elements and cultural elements mix together and interact together. The interactors coming from various cultural backgrounds have different preferences and requirements toward a specific language act in a certain situation. For instance, the most important thing to reflect American people's value is probably their devotion to "individualism", which is the core of American social life. According to the idea of individualism, the rights and freedom of the individual are the most important rights in society. An individual's privacy and independence are regarded as divine and inviolable. As for the Chinese people, they tend to show too much concern over other people's business. If we can't keep these differences in our minds, we may commit some unnecessary mistakes while communicating with foreigners.

A: You look pale. What's the matter?

B: I'm feeling sick. A cold, may be.

A: Go and see the doctor. Drink more water. Did you take any pills? Then put on more clothes. Have a good rest.

B: You are not my mother, are you?

Apparently, B's last reply sounds unpleasant. The reason is that A seems over-warm. His care for B's health is so superfluous that B nearly takes it as an offence against his independence. As a matter of fact, if he speaks in this way "Take care of yourself. I hope you will be better soon."

that is more proper. Thus, we conclude that cultural differences will certainly lead to pragmatic differences. These pragmatic differences have a direct impact on language communication. As result, people from different cultures may easily get into troubles—unnecessary misunderstandings or conflicts.

To a large extent the success of intercultural communication depends on our ability to forge good links with the local personnel, to understand what Holliday calls their "real world problem" and to have some insights into the surface and deep action of the institutional culture. In communicating with people from different cultures, on the one hand, we ought to command the linguistic knowledge (phonetics, lexicology, grammar). On the other hand, it is necessary for us to have a better understanding and knowledge as to the difference between source language culture and target language culture and their pragmatic differences.

Generally speaking, culturalpragmatic differences play an important role in the process of intercultural communication in such aspects as greetings, thanks and compliments, and terms of address.

3.3.1 Greetings

It's a common practice for English-speaking people to greet friends every time when they meet during the day. Thus the same greeting "How are you?" may be spoken many times a day to the same friend, which seems to be redundant and hence unnecessary to a Chinese speaker. Both the Chinese and the English express greetings in their unique way. If one doesn't know the differences in greeting people, he can't even start a conversation or he may put himself at the risk of causing misunderstandings and even embarrassment. The following examples are very typical.

A Chinese student ran into his foreign teacher somewhere. They greeted each other:

Student: Hello.

Foreign teacher: Hi, how are you?

Student: Fine. How are you getting on?

Foreign teacher: (in a confusing voice) Just so so.

"How are you getting on?" implies that the speaker has already known what things the hearer is doing. Therefore, it is not proper to use such an expression as a greeting when a person sees the other for the first time of the day. It's better to say, "Fine, and how are you?"

Usually, a Chinese speaker greets an American from the distance "I am afraid you must have had a tiring journey."（你一路辛苦了）This is correct in grammar and semantic rules, but the better greeting is "Did you have a good trip?" "Did you enjoy your trip?" "How was trip?" or "You must have a tolerable trip."

The Chinese always use very specific questions in greeting to show their consideration for other people. Such questions as "Where are you going?" "Where have you just been?" do not really ask for information. Instead, they are used as greetings. This has nothing to do with offence. Such questions in the English culture, however, are normally requests for information. Such details are considered as personal affairs and thus, these questions can typically be used by someone in authority or between very close friends. When the English people are greeted by these questions, they are forced into a dilemma: they don't know how to deal with these greetings. To reply vaguely or honestly is always hard to decide. So native English speakers may easily be offended at such Chinese forms of greetings and regard them as invasions of their privacy.

When English-speaking people meet for the first time during the day, they often say something like "How are you?" "How are you doing?" "Hello" "How is life?" These forms of greetings suggest that native speakers of English use very general questions to greet people instead of using very specific questions as we Chinese do. This is just because the English people pay more respect to other's privacy. Each person expects his own rights to be recognized, and then he respects other's rights. The English people, therefore, would not like to ask or be asked about personal matters in order to avoid an invasion of privacy.

3.3.2　Thanks and Compliments

It is noted that people in the English culture tend to express their gratitude and compliments more than the Chinese speakers and accordingly they tend to accept thanks and compliments more than we Chinese. In China people seldom praise their own family members before guests while the English people often take an opposite attitude. The remark "Your wife is really beautiful" would be regarded as almost indecent by many Chinese. Yet the same compliment would be considered perfectly natural and even highly appreciated by the English people.

In response to compliments, English people tend to accept them while the Chinese generally deny the praise. When a native English speaker expresses to us his gratitude, we may feel embarrassed and would sometimes say "no, no" to decline whatever expressions of gratitude. However, an English speaker in a similar situation, would say something like "I am glad to hear it" or "I am glad to be of help" to acknowledge and accept the thanks. To the Chinese speakers, expressions like "Not at all" or "It's nothing" used by the English people to turn down thanks may not sound emphatic enough.

Similarly, many Chinese speakers feel embarrassed when they hear compliments like "You speak excellent English." To show they do not deserve a compliment, they tend to use an emphatic "No". A young girl was once complimented by her English boss "That is a lovely dress you have on." In response to it, the girl said, "No, no. It's just an ordinary one." The answer suggests that the girl laughs at her boss. It seems that her English boss has no appreciation of good dress. According to the Chinese culture, it is polite and decent to maximize the disparise of self and minimize the praise of self. But such a response in the above example has far exceeded the foreigner's understanding of modesty. That foreigner might think that the Chinese girl was impolite to respond with immediate and repeated denials instead of thanks.

When the English people thank a person for paying them a compliment, generally they thank the person, not because they necessarily agree with the compliment, but because they think that the person is kind enough to take the time to do so. They do this just to maximize benefit to the other and maximize agreement between self and the other.

3.3.3 Terms of Address

There are two main forms of addresses: addresses among the family members and addresses in communication with others. Generally, the Chinese system of forms of address has been dominated by status and politeness norms. It is polite to address each other according to the traditional order of hierarchy. Terms such as "uncle, aunt, grandpa, granny" are used as honorific titles for strangers, as in "Uncle Li, Aunt Ma". In addition, the Chinese often use professional titles to address others. Such respectful titles as Chairman Li, Director Wang are often used to indicate people's influential status, which is typical of the Chinese culture.

An English lady, Helen, was invited to visit a school in China. On entering into the school, a group of pupils came up to her.

Helen: Hello.

Pupils: Hello, Aunty. Hello, Aunty.

Helen: (embarrassed)

We can imagine the reactions of Miss Helen. It's just because the pupils don't know the English people are not used to being called with kin addressing.

In Western countries, the title-plus-last name structure is used for formal discourse situation. In an informal and friendly setting, Westerners expect to be called by their first name. First names are also required for use between people who work closely together. Addressing others by using the first name is especially common among Americans, even when people meet for the first time. It is not at all uncommon to hear a child calls a much older person—Ben, Joe, Helen, etc. This may even include the child's parents. In China, there are deep prohibitions against the expression of intimacy outside the family circle and that of close friends.

第 3 章　语用失误的理论综述

在语用学的范畴中,有关语用失误的理论涉及面比较广,包括 Austin 的言语行为理论、Searle 的间接言语行为理论、Grice 的合作原则,以及 Leech 和 Gu Yueguo 的礼貌原则。在基于这些理论的基础上,许多涉及语用失误的例证将会被大量引用和分析。笔者也集中分析了在语言交流过程中的语用差异,这种差异来源于文化多样性,而且会对交际失误有直接影响。

3.1　语用学的理论思考

在进一步探索语用失误的本质之前,我们最好能对语用学视角进行大体的了解。根据 Verschueren 的观点,将语用学定义为在语言现象中的一种总体认知、社会和文化观,以行为的形式,与实际的使用相互联系。还有一些语言学家们将其定义为合乎语法规则,或是在语言结构中,具有编码性质的语言和语言使用环境之间的研究。何自然的观点如下所述:语用学研究了在特定情境下的表达方式,即如何通过情景理解和使用语言。

在跨文化交际的过程中,语用原则的掌握在很大程度上与语言正确恰当的使用相互关联,对减少语用失误也有很大帮助。因为语用原则有普遍性以及社会、文化相对性的特点,所以我们会通过采用语用学理论中的一些观点,对语用失误进行分析。

3.1.1　指示特征

就语言自身结构而言,总能唯一展现语言和语境关系而且最显然的方法在于指示词方面。本质上而言,指示词主要用来表示对话的参与者,对话发生的空间、时间以及社会环境。特定的指示词表达取决于上下文。指示信息对于话语理解的重要性可能完美地展现于指示信息缺失的时候。让我们看以下句子。

（1）I'll be back in half an hour. 如果孤立地或者不参照任何上下文地翻译这个句子，我们会看到这个句子没有传递任何信息。因为我们不知道该句子是什么时候写下来的，我们也就无从得知作者何时会回来。或者，想象一下熄灯时 Hamy 正开始说以下句子。

（2）Listen, I'm not disagreeing with you but with you, and not about this but about this. 我们不知道"你"指的是谁；并且"这个"指什么也没有上下文知识。所有这些表达的理解都取决于说话者和倾听者所共处的相同的语言环境。如果有人对你面对面地说"I'll arrive tomorrow morning"，那么你对他什么时候到毫无疑问。但是如果一个粗心的人从另一个半球给你发来电报"arrive 11:00 am tomorrow"，你可能就会对其真正到达的时间非常费解。问题在于时差的存在。在中国的人们和在美国的人们对于"明天"和"上午 11点"有着不同的认识。因此我们必须具有一个清楚的参照点以此来理解指示代词。在语言交流中，这个参照点就在于说话者。位处交流中心的人正是说话者。因此非常清晰的是说话者所说的时间是指示中心，说话者说话时所在地是谈话的中心地。因此，语言中的指示项以说话者为基础而组织起来。

以上的论述主要是关于指示性用法，也就是指示词的指示对象以及其暗指随上下文的改变而改变。指示词传统分类为人物、地点和时间。在对人物性指示词的研究中，经常用"I am in the last place"来暗指说话者是最后一名。但是这个句子也用于一些场合以指明其他某人是最后一名。例如，你在观看一场比赛，你所下注的二号选手落到了最后一名。"I am in the last place!"你对你的同伴生气的吼道。你的同伴自然非常清楚你所表达的意思——你所下注的选手是最后一名而不是你。甚至他会友好地反驳你。"No, you aren't. Look, you are passing No.3!"这种交流的成功一定是经历在一定的语境当中的，否则必定会引起误会。

一些内置指示成分的动作词值得我们深思。英语中，"come"和"go"在言语活动参与者相关的动作的所指上有一定的区别。我们能够注意到，就汉语理解而言，"他来了"似乎意味着"他朝着说话人所在地移动过来了，而"他走了"则意为"他正在远离说话人所在地"。据此解释，"I'm coming to London"似乎是不合逻辑的。但是英语中，有这样一个习惯用法——当说话人动作的目的地与听者一致时，指示中心在听者一方而非说话者。这可能是一种礼貌，因此，当朝向听者移动时，我们用"来"。实践中，夹着一个中国学生和他或者她的同学约定去拜访他。在此案列中，我们应当说"Can I come to your home tomorrow?"而不是"Can I go to your home tomorrow?"

就时间指示性词来说,我们注意到诸如"yesterday""today"和"tomorrow"这些指示词占据着历法或者纯粹指代有关日子的方式。有趣的是,以英语为母语的人也习惯于使用它们。在先入为主的规则如下,指代相同时间时,我们倾向于使用更加一般的、不确定的时间指示词而非绝对的时间性指示词。让我们比较以下一组句子:

(1)I'm going to leave here on Thursday.

(2)I'm going to leave here today.

(3) I'm going to leave here tomorrow.

如果"今天"是周四,英语国家人们倾向于使用(2)。如果"今天"是周三,他们可能用(3)而非(1)。如果我们仍坚持使用(1),则"周四"只能指代下周四(或者是更远的周四)。一些时候,英语和汉语就时间指示词的表达并不相同。如果一个说英语的人说"It will be held next Thursday",则"next Thursday"等同于汉语中的"下周的周四",其条件是当前说话时间是从周三到周天。如果当前时间是周一或者周二,歧义就产生了。"下个周四"既可以指这周四又可以指九天或者十天后的那个周四。

由此可见,指示性表达的解释取决于上下文语境和说话者的动机。指示性表达总传递比其自身更多的信息。指示性词成为人类交流的一个共性特征。从互动角度出发,就能够注意到,指示性表达有时具有文化特殊性。在研究语用错误中,我们建议应在这方面投入更多的精力。

3.1.2　言语行为

一般的语用理论当中所有的议题中,言语行为理论可能引发了最广泛的兴趣。该理论研究的是一个词汇或一个句子在特定的语境中所产生的交际功能。

为了将其表述出来,人们不仅引入了包含语法句法结构和词汇的表达,并且通过这些表达方式采取相应的行为。通过话语表达所采取的行为一般称之为言语行为。言语行为普遍被贴上了更特殊的标签,如道歉、抱怨、恭维、邀请、承诺或者请求。这些言语行为适用于产生一个话语过程中的说话者交流意图。

无论什么情况下,产生一个话语的行为包含三个相关联的行为。Austin分离出三种基本的感官,用来说明一些人在做某事时,因此三种行为也就同时发生了。

(1)言内行为:具有确定意义和所指的句子话语。

(2)言外行为:通过与之相关的常规力量(或以其明确的演示释义)来发表

一个句子的陈述,提供承诺等。

(3)言后行为:话语环境所产生的特殊后果。

Austin 论述的核心是"说话就是信服"。在跨文化交流中,言外行为和言后行为通常是我们兴趣点所在。优势说话者的言外行为不能充分地被听众所理解。因此就会形成一些歧义。因而,也无法满意地达到言后行为以至于说话者言语行为的表达意图与其效果截然相反。所以,我们必须比较和分析话语行为的运行过程以及就不同文化背景而言的相关语用错误。

(4)在关于英语课堂的讨论中,英语教师 X 先生告诉其学生,他的妻子 X 夫人将不会参加来到教室和大家一同讨论了,他对此表示非常抱歉。随后,一个中国学生说到他自己:"Like Mrs X, I've also caught a very bad cold, yet I have to come to class.",这时候,X 先生打断了该学生的话,并说道:"But you have a very tough constitution."。

我们可以清楚地看到,X 先生的回复是解释性且被迫性的。其学生的陈述对 X 先生的思维、感情和行为都有着消极的影响。这就是一种言后行为,会让 X 先生尴尬不已。而在学生的角度上,他只是关注陈述即便和 X 女士一样得了重感冒,他依旧来上课了这样一件事情。学生陈述的结果是一种言外之意。对于 X 先生而言,学生讲其自身同 X 女士联系在一起,并好奇为什么 X 女士没能像他一样来上课。理所当然的我们不难理解为什么 X 先生会如此不耐烦地为自己辩解。

(5)在一节翻译课上,X 先生在检查他几天前给学生们布置的任务。他让学生读出他们修改后的译文用于深入的讨论。

Mr X:Miss A, did you revise your own version?

Miss A:No, I didn't. I still stick to my original version. I think it is too soon to do it.

Mr X:You think your original version is perfect.

Miss A:...

在这个对话中,X 先生想让 A 小姐读出她修改后的译文。这个语言行为的基础是他认为学生们会负责任地完成他们的作业。当他说到,"Did you revise your own version?"他没有询问学生是否完成了作业。在其言内行为中,他所要强调的仅仅是给出一个温和的指令。而 A 小姐则误解了他的要求。她只是将其想当然地理解为 X 先生话语的言外行为是检查她的作业。当然她的回复被 X 先生拒绝了。虽然 A 小姐没有故意地反驳 X 先生,然而语用错误还是发生了。关键点在于 A 小姐错解了 X 先生话语的言外之意。在此环境下,X 先生话语的言后行为产生了这样一种效果,即 A 小姐非常焦虑以至于不得不立即为自己辩解。如果她充分地了解交流功能和言语行为的语用意义,一些错误或者尴尬的僵局在一定程度上就可以得以避免。从某种意义上来说,A 小姐的回答可以这样进行改善:"Perhaps in a day or two when I look at it again,I'll change my mind."

(6)在一趟火车上,当列车停止的时候一个中国人脑袋撞到了窗户上,看到这幅场景,邻座的美国人对此表示非常遗憾:

American:I am sorry.

Chinese:It's not your fault.

这个对话中发生了语用错误。当美国人说"I am sorry"的时候,其言外之意是为了向中国人表达同情。但是中国人却将这种同情误解为了道歉。因此,美国人对这样的回答疑惑不已。

Searle 认为,言语行为能够实现在不同的社会和文化背景下对于话语的多维度意义,然而,特定的和独有的社会传统和文化规范将是判定说话者所要传达和听话者所接收到的准确信息关键所在。许多情况下,跨文化交际活动陷入僵局都是因为文化背景的差异。

人际交往中打招呼起着非常重要的作用。打招呼是交流的开端,如果我们不能妥当地使用,交流进程很可能就此打断。我们中国人相互打招呼经常是这样:"你出去啊?"或者是"你上哪儿去?"。在中国文化中,这些话的言外之意或效果仅仅是互相客套的打招呼。但是如果我们对一个美国人说"Where are you going?",原本的言外之意将会丧失,言外行为也不会被感知。相反,美国人也会想当然地认为"Where are you going?"的言外之意是你想询问他(她)的隐私。在这种情况下,预期的言后行为肯定也就不会发生了。此时,交流活动就此结束。

在不同的文化环境下,拒绝或者排斥的表达反映了不同文化的内涵。拒绝某人或者排斥某人就中国传统文化而言,一定程度上暗指着不礼貌或者无理。换言之,中国人的言语行为受限于"礼貌原则"并维系在"面子活儿"上。当拒绝他人时,中国人通常尝试巧妙地间接地去解释以免伤了别人的"脸面"。但是在西方文化中,"保留脸面"这一概念并不存在。许多英语国家人会对中国人所提出的"丢脸"非常疑惑。一个美国商人与中国商人就投资问题的一些重要方面进行谈判,随后,他想知道自己的项目是否被接受了。中国商人只是重复着中国老话"We'll think this over again.""We must give it more thought."实际上,中国商人所要表达的就是"No,we don't agree with your proposal."但是美国人并不能认识到表示"不认同"的言外之意。他想当然地认为对方迟早会重新考虑他的提议。所以美国人等待着中国人给他回复,结果自然也是不言自明的。言后行为的效果与中国人期许的不尽相同。我们从这个案例中发现英语文化中拒绝的表达更加直接了当。相反,中国人对拒绝的表达则更为间接并且言内行为的"意义"与言外行为的"意义"并不一致,有时他们也截然相反。

就赞美的言语行为而言,一些赞美的言外行为可被看作暗含了一些其他的意图。例如,当一个英国人向以为中国女士表达了"You are attractive."这样的赞美,其言外行为充当了表扬这一功能,言后行为是意图使其高兴开心。但是这位中国女士的反应的特点就是尴尬的脸红。因为在中国,陌生男人对女士美貌的赞美会被认为是不合适的轻佻的行为。恭维女士外表是中国人的一大禁忌。因此在中国文化背景下,这样的赞美性话语并不会带来理想的结果,反而使其尴尬不已。

3.1.3　间接话语行为

根据 Searle 的论述,大多数情况下,言语行为是通过另外一个言语行为间接进行的。他指出,说话者通常通过明确做出另外一种言外行为来含蓄地进行言外行为。明确执行的行为用于传达另一种言语行为;说话者依靠其与听众所分享的背景知识和心理能力达到理解。

对于大多数间接言语行为,必须拥有不同的触发器,也就是一些暗示,这些暗示表明字面意义在某些语境中是不充分的,需要进行一些"修正"。看以下对话:

(1) A：Let's go to the movie tonight.

B：I have to study for the exam.

B 的回答传递着这样的信息:我恐怕今晚不能和你一起去。结果就是,A 乐意地接受了这个拒绝。但是如果双方没有共同的知识或背景,B 的话语中所谓表达出来的信息可能就不会被 A 所理解。有时候,由于缺乏共同的知识,听众对于一个间接话语行为的理解可能与其言外行为不一致。

(2) Aunt：Won't you have another piece of cake,Tommy?

Tommy：No,I thank you.

Aunt：You seem to be suffering from loss of appetite.

Tommy：That isn't loss of appetite. What I'm suffering from is politeness.

当 Tommy 回答"No, I thank you"的时候, 一种间接的言外之意油然而生。Tommy 和阿姨之间缺乏一种共同的知识。阿姨只是字面地理解了 Tommy 的拒绝。她没能理解 Tommy 的言外之意是已经准备好阿姨再让给他一块儿蛋糕了。他没有直接地表达自己的意思, 因为他认为在他阿姨面前会有些奇怪陌生。这个例子展现了在某种特出情况或场合下, 如果说话人和听众之间缺乏语境条件或背景信息, 那么采用间接的语言行为就不合适了。

在我们日常生活中, 如果一个人要去拜访他的朋友或同事, 以下对话可能经常发生在一个中国家庭里。

（3）Host：It's getting dark. I suppose you haven't had your supper yet. Stay with us and have a dinner.

Guest：It doesn't matter. I have already finished.

在这个谈话中, 主人话语的言外行为并没有反映主人对客人的关照。而是暗示着"你该回去了"。不走运的是, 客人没有理解主人的言外之意, 结果就是客人的回答听起来不那么合适。

（4）A tourist guide led a group of English people to the coach. The driver didn't turn on the air-conditioner, so it is very hot and sultry inside the coach. One tourist said：

Tourist：Oh, it reminds me of my Vesuvius tour（威苏威火山之旅）last summer.

Guide：Oh, you've traveled a lot.

实际上, 游客话语的言外之意是暗示了一种不满和要求, 也就是说"It is too hot here. Is it possible that the driver turns on the air - conditioner a bit earlier?"。但是导游只明白了字面意, 因此造成了误解。

3.1.4　合作原则

Grice 的言外之意概念本质上是一个论述人们如何使用语言的概念。他认为一个对话中涉及的人都要相互合作。Grice 确定了有效合作使用语言的四个基本要素, 共同表达了一般的合作原则。

（1）合作原则。按照您所参与的谈话的目的或方向, 在会话进行的阶段做出相应的贡献。

（2）质量准则。试图让你的贡献是真实的，具体来说：

a.不要说你所认为是假的信息。

b.不要说缺乏足够证据的信息。

（3）数量准则。

a.只说当前交际目的所需的信息。

b.不要使你的信息比需要的信息更多。

（4）中肯准则。

a.使你的信息中肯。

（5）礼貌准则。明了明确：

a.避免晦涩。

b.避免模棱两可。

c.简短。

d.有序。

简而言之，这些标准给我们的建议是，当提供充分信息时，应该真诚中肯清晰。否则，交流可能就不会流畅地进行。

（6）A.Can you tell me how to make egg soup?

B.I have a recipe that got from my aunt.

A.(Puzzled) You didn't answer my question.

这里 A 感到疑惑的原因是他没有考虑到和关联准则相关的 B 的话语的言外之意。然而 B 在其回答中运用了关联准则，意思是"I could offer you my aunt's recipe."由于 A 没有遵循合作原则，交流失败了。

跨文化交际过程可能得以有效进行是由于参与者遵循这些原则。但是，由于参与者自身不同的文化，这些原则可能不会被完全一致地遵循。一个外籍教师询问他能否被允许去观摩中国教师的课堂。系主任跟他的谈话如下：

（7）Foreign teacher：I'd like to visit Miss Ma's class. Will that be all right?

Dean：I'm sure you understand our problems. Because of certain reasons, it may not be possible.

这里系主任给外教的间接回复违反了数量标准，产生了会话的言外之意。这让外教对其要求的可行性和适当性更加疑惑。在中国文化中，大量的信息是通过理解而非字面得来的，而从字面得到大量信息又是典型的英语国家的方式。所以最好这样说:"I'll have to tell Miss Ma but I doubt it."

　　在讲汉语的语境中,社会距离和社会关系是相对稳定的,社会地位较低的说话者被那些拥有较高社会地位的人所影响并且会顺从于他们。在这种情况下,他们对于四个准则的遵守程度就和西方人大有不同。相对而言,中国说话者似乎更注重"礼貌准则"而非"质量"和"数量"准则。通常,当中国人被邀请吃晚餐或者被劝吃些东西,他们习惯性会说"No, it is no need."。中国文化中,这应该理解为"好啊,再邀请我一次"。但是对于美国人而言,这是明显的拒绝。当拒绝他人时,中国人不说"不"而更倾向于使用模糊性话语。比如"我们研究研究""可能不方便吧",等等。这些回答似乎模棱两可,这也因此违背了 Grice 的质量、数量和中肯准则。但是对于汉语母语者而言,这听起来更礼貌、自然。对于英语为母语的人,他们通常会对他们所看到的感到非常困惑并且非常恼怒,因为他们认为这是对其正面请求的逃避。

3.2　跨文化语用对比分析

　　语用错误产生于文化差别是现实存在的。实际上,不同文化背景的人们对一些与对话和交流相关的理论和规则持有不同的理解和认识。所以,许多错误就此产生。从这个意义上来说,对跨文化交际中的这些理论和原则进行对比学习是非常有必要的。

3.2.1　中英文化中的礼貌性原则

　　由于不同的文化背景和价值观,中国人和西方人对礼貌有着不同的标准。在这里将介绍和比较两种礼貌性理论。一个是 Geoffrey Leech,他基于英语社会建立该理论;另外一个是顾曰国,其理论具有汉语社会特点。

　　Geoffrey Leech 列举了以下几个基本的礼貌性原则:

　　(1)得体准则(在指令性和许诺性话语中)。

　　a. 最小化牺牲他人。

　　b. 最大化惠及他人。

　　(2)慷慨准则(在指令性和许诺性话语中)。

　　a. 最小化惠及自己。

　　b. 最大化牺牲自己。

　　(3)赞扬准则(用于表达和态度)。

a. 尽量缩小对别人的贬低。

b. 尽量赞扬别人。

（4）谦虚准则（用于表达和态度）。

a. 尽量减小对自己的表扬。

b. 尽量贬低自己。

（5）赞同准则（用于说明态度）。

a. 尽量缩小自己与他人的分歧。

b. 增强自己与他人的共识。

（6）同情准则（用于说明态度）。

a. 尽量减少自己对别人的厌恶。

b. 增加对别人的同情。

然而，在现实生活中，中国人与英国人对此的理解相差甚远。中国文化中所体现的客气行为在英国人看来恰恰相反，是不礼貌的。以得体准则和慷慨准则为例。一位中国主人坚持要给美国客人沏一杯茶，说到"Have a cup of tea"并立刻沏了杯茶。即使客人说自己并不想喝，主人也会再三请求并说类似于"You must have a taste."或"You must drink some."当他们向客人提供食物时，中国人也同样会展示出自己的热情与真诚，这使得客人感到很不舒服。中国人认为他的这种提供食物行为会尽可能地使客人受益而减少自身的利益。但他没有意识到自己的这种热情慷慨的过分要求使客人的自主权、自由独立行为受到了限制。这样的话，越是热情，客人会越不高兴。

与 Leech 的礼貌原则相反，顾曰国总结出的中国人的礼貌原则，其特点是尊重、谦虚、热情和文雅。并规定了以下五项准则。

（1）贬己尊人准则：指谈到自己或与自己相关的事物时要"贬"，要"谦"；谈到听者或者与听者相关的事物时要"抬"，要"尊"。

（2）称呼准则：对双方的称呼要依据传统社会级别次序来表明双方在交流中的人际关系。

（3）文雅准则：使用间接语而不是直接用语，使语言听起来更文雅。

（4）求同准则：说话双方力求和谐一致。

（5）德言行准则：在行为动机上尽量减少他人付出的代价，尽量增加他人的利益；在言辞上尽量夸大别人对自己的好处，尽量说小自己付出的代价。

受文化背景和价值观念的影响，礼貌原则中也不可能不受别国文化的影响。以下会分析一些不同文化交流过程中存在的与礼貌原则相关的语用失误实例。

（1）一位中国人正在跟他的美国朋友在一家餐厅吃饭。

American：I enjoy the meal very much.

Chinese：Taste this, eat slowly, eat more.

在中国文化中，这位中国人的行为是得体大方的表现。但同样的行为在外国文化中是不得体的。纵然使对方的利益最大化了，但却冒犯了对方的独立和自由。吃多少是对方自己的选择。而且一次吃太多也是不得体的，所以中国人最好这样说"Help yourself, please."否则，美国人觉得中国人是独断专横的。

（2）一位美国经理这样表扬他的员工。

American manager：You have done a wonderful job.

Chinese employee：No, no. I didn't do it very well.

谦虚是中国文化中一个显著的特点，然而美国人们却不这样认为。中国文化中的谦虚总是把自己放得很低，把别人抬得很高。然而，Leech 主张的礼貌原则里的"谦虚"是避免自夸。中国文化中的谦虚是汉语礼貌原则的核心，而谦虚准则在 Leech 的礼貌原则里却没有那么重要。中国文化里的谦虚是提高自身修养的一种好品质，是礼貌待人的基础；而英语中的谦虚是尽量不要自夸。这就是为什么英语为母语的人总是很难理解汉语中表达谦虚时所说的一些不太好听的话。

一位美国教授讲完课后跟一位中国老师进行交流。这位中国老师对他说，"You look rather tired. You had better take a good rest."在交际中，中国人考虑更多的是他人。但有时中国人大多误用了同情准则。同情准则的意思是需要体会理解他人的感受。表达出你的同情的同时也要避免他人反感。倘若不知道如何避免反感，那就可能在中国人和与英语为母语的人交流的过程中产生严重的交流失败现象。中国人在说话时总是为对方考虑得更多些。他们认为任何为他人着想的表达都是礼貌的。这样，这位中国老师就说出了尊重和关心他的话。这与中国文化中的同情准则是一致的。但在英语文化中，这位外国教授想到的可能是这位中国老师对他的课不满意，所以话里蕴含着批判的意思。这已经远远超出了美国人对同情准则的理解，在他们认为这是非常不礼貌的。

而且，在中国和英国文化中，得体准则都有所体现，只是两种文化对此是用不同的方式来理解的。一位美国人邀请一位中国人时说到"Would you join us for dinner tonight?"这位中国人回答道："No，thanks. It would be too much trouble for you."这个回答常让美国人出乎意料。事实上,双方也都遵守了自己的得体准则。美国人认为邀请这位中国人吃饭使自己的利益最小化而使这位中国朋友的利益最大化,但这位中国朋友的没有充分理由的回绝让美国人看来是不礼貌的,违反了他国文化中的得体准则。然而,对于中国人来说,他可能想着自己受损最小的同时给美国人带来麻烦,才在接受别人的好处前多次推辞,这在中国文化中是公认的礼貌行为。

3.3　语言交际中的语用差异

虽然交际任务中的语用情景从理论上来说是广泛适用的,但在实际的社交中不同的文化表现不一。语言的交流是一个语言和文化共同交织融合的过程。来自不同文化背景的因素相互作用使得在同一语境中不同文化有不同的喜好和要求。例如,最能反映美国人价值观的就是他们推崇的"个人主义",这是美国社会生活的核心思想。从个人主义来看,在美国社会里权利和自由是最重要的。个人的隐私和独立是神圣不容侵犯的。对于中国人来说,他们更倾向于关心别人的事情。如果不把这些文化差异记在心中,那么当我们跟外国朋友交流时可能就会犯一些不必要的错误。

A：You look pale. What's the matter?

B：I'm feeling sick. A cold，may be.

A：Go and see the doctor. Drink more water. Did you take any pills? Then put on more clothes. Have a good rest.

B：You are not my mother，are you?

很显然,B 最后的回答听起来不太高兴。这说明 A 似乎有点热情过头了。他对 B 健康的关心是多余的,以至于要触犯他的独立性。事实上,如果他说"Take care of yourself. I hope you will be better soon."更合适。因此,我们总结出这么一点:文化差异必然导致语用时的差异。这些语用差异对语言交流有着直接的影响。不同国家的人可能会陷入一些不必要的误会和争吵中。

不同文化之间的成功交流很大程度上取决于达成双方良好关系的能力,正确理解 Holliday 所说的"现实问题"的能力以及对已有文化的表面和实质意思的理解能力。在跟外国朋友交流时,一方面,我们应该遵照语言知识(语音学,词汇学,语法);另一方面,我们应该对源语言和目标语言在文化和语用方面的差异有充分的认识和理解。

一般而言,像在表达问候,感谢,赞美及称谓语时,语用文化差异在不同文化交流过程中起着非常重要的作用。

3.3.1 问候语

讲英语的人每次白天碰见友人时都要进行问候。同样的问候语"How are you?"可能一天对一个朋友都说过很多次,这对中国人来说似乎是多余不必的。英国人和中国人在表达问候时方式不同。一个人如果不懂问候方式的差异性,他甚至无法开始对话或者是使自己陷入被误解的泥潭进而尴尬难堪。下面的这个例子就特别典型。

一位中国学生跑到他的外教跟前。他们互相问候对方:

Student:Hello.

Foreign teacher:Hi,how are you?

Student:Fine. How are you getting on?

Foreign teacher:(in a confusing voice) Just so so.

How are you getting on? 这句话意味着说话人已经知道听话者最近的动态。因此,当第一次遇见一个人时这样问候对方是不恰当的。这样说更恰当:"Fine,and how are you?"

一般情况下,中国人会对远道而来的外国朋友说"I am afraid you must have had a tiring journey."(你一路辛苦了)这在语法和句法上都没错,但更好的表达是这样的"Did you have a good trip?""Did you enjoy your trip?""How was trip?"或者"You must have a tolerable trip."

中国人在问候时用具体的问题表达对他人的关心。诸如"去哪儿呢?""去哪儿了?"这些问题没有问些具体的信息。相反,它们被用作问候语。这也不冒犯他人。然而这在英国文化中,问这些问题就不太恰当了。这些琐事被看成是自己的私事,也只有有权利对自己过问的人和非常亲密的朋友才能提及。当英国人打招呼时被问到这些问题时,他们会身陷困境,左右为难,不知如何开口回答这些问题。到底是给个模糊的回答呢还是如实回答总是那么的难做决定。所以以英语为母语的人可能会觉得这种汉语式的打招呼是对他们隐私的侵犯。

当英国人白天初次见面时,时常会说"How are you?""How are you doing?""Hello""How is life?"这些打招呼的方式表明英国人打招呼的方式刚好与中国人相反,就是问下大概而不是细节。这就是因为英国人更尊重他人的隐私。每个人都意识到自己应有的权利,也会尊重他人的权利。所以,为了避免侵犯他人隐私,英国人不喜欢谈及自己或他人的事情。

3.3.2 感谢语和赞美语

据说与中国人相比,英国人多会把自己的感激之情和赞美之意表达出来,同样他们也更容易接受别人的感恩和赞扬。在中国,人们几乎不在客人面前赞扬自己的家人,然而英国人对此持相反态度。一句"Your wife is really beautiful",这样的评价多会被中国人视为下流低级。然而,同样的评价被英国人视为是很自然极度欣赏对方的评价。

对于别人的称赞,英国人多是接受;然而,中国人通常会否定对方的夸赞。当英国人向我们表达他的感激时,我们可能会觉得尴尬,用"不,不"这样的回答来婉言谢绝对方的感激之情。然而,英国人在这种情况下将会回答"I am glad to hear it"或"I am glad to be of help"来接受对方的谢意。对于中国人来说,英国人用像"Not at all"或"It's nothing"这样的话来谢绝让人觉得可能太唐突或强硬。

同样,当一些中国人听到"You speak excellent English"这样的称赞时,很多人都会感到尴尬。为了表明自己不值得称赞,他们多会生硬地说出"No"。一位年轻的姑娘曾被她的英国老板这样夸道:"That is a lovely dress you have on."这位女孩这样回答道:"No, no. It's just an ordinary one."这样的回答暗示着这位女孩在嘲笑她的老板。貌似她的英国老板不懂欣赏衣服。根据中国文化,贬低自我,夸奖他人是礼貌的。但以上例子中的回答远远超出了外国人对谦虚的理解。外国人会觉得这个中国女孩如此快速且多次否定而不是给予感谢的回答是不礼貌的。

当英国人对一个人出于感谢而发出赞美的声音时,通常他们感谢一个人,不是因为他们认同赞扬的必要性,而是因为他们认为这个人足够和蔼而值得这样做。他们这样做仅仅是为了使他人的利益最大化,增强自己与他人的共识。

3.3.3 称谓语

称谓语有两种最主要的形式：一种是家庭成员之间的称呼,另一种是对他人交流时的称呼。一般来说,中国的称呼方式这一系统是由地位身份和礼貌用语决定的。根据传统的长幼次序来称呼对方是有礼貌的表现。像"叔叔、姨姨、爷爷、奶奶"这些词语用在陌生人的前面表尊称。另外,中国人用职业头衔来称呼他人。像李主席、王导演,都被用来提示对方的重要身份,这就是中国文化的特点。

一位英国妇女,Helen 被邀请去参观一所中国学校。一进学校,一群小学生就凑了上来。

Helen：Hello.

Pupils：Hello, Aunty. Hello, Aunty.

Helen：(embarrassed)

我们能想象出 Helen 当时的反应如何。仅是因为小学生不知道如何友好地称呼英国人。

在西方国家,头衔加姓这样的名字结构用在正式场合的交谈中。在友好的非正式的交谈中,西方人希望别人叫他们的名字。工作伙伴也要求叫对方的名字。美国人在第一次见面时通常更多地是叫别人的名字。听到小孩子给年长的人叫 Ben, Joe, Helen 等很普遍。这也可能包括孩子父母。在中国,出了家门是绝不允许用亲昵的称呼,甚至很亲密的朋友。

CHAPTER 4   PRAGMATIC FAILURES IN INTERCULTURAL COMMUNICATION

Leech and Levinson behieved, Pragmatics covers a wide stretch of territory. However, from the viewpoint of intercultural encounters, what is particularly relevant to pragmatic failures or miscommunication is the link pragmatics makes between the ways that communicative behavior is performed and the ongoing understandings of people in interaction. In order to analyze pragmatic failures, we should have a better understanding about the notion of sociocultural knowledge, the extralinguistic knowledge of culture and the world that is often revealed in communicative behavior.

4.1   Categories of Pragmatic Failures

Miller points out that most of our misunderstandings of other people are not due to any inability to hear them or to parse their sentences or to understand their words. A far more important source of difficulty in the process of intercultural communication is that we often fail to understand the speaker's intention. Jenny Thomas defines the term "pragmatic failure" as "the inability to understand what is meant by what is said".

Pragmatic failure is an area of intercultural communication breakdown. Thomas chosses the term "pragmatic failure" rather than "pragmatic error" in that unlike linguistic errors which can be prescribed by strict grammar rules, pragmatic competence includes probable rather than categorical rules. Therefore it may be inappropriate to say that the pragmatic force or meaning of an utterance is "wrong", but rather it fails to achieve the speaker's purpose. Two types of cross-cultural pragmatic failures are identified: pragmalinguistic failures and sociopragmatic failures.

4.1.1　The Necessity to Distinguish Pragmalinguistic Failures from Sociopragmatic Failures

Pragmalinguistic failure is basically a linguistic problem, which is caused by differences in the linguistic encoding of pragmatic force; sociopragmatic failure stems from cross-culturally different perceptions of what constitutes appropriate linguistic behavior. In order to interpret the force of an utterance in the way in which a speaker intends, the hearer must take into account both contextual and linguistic cues. Often, context alone will determine what force is assigned to an utterance. It is true in every culture that the implicatures of speech illocutions are dependent on some particular context, so any utterance could be implicated unambiguously only with given appropriate contextual cues that are shared by cultural knowledge or experience of speaker and hearer, or association clues that are provided by mentioning something associated with the act required of hearer, either by precedent in speaker-hearer's experience or by mutual knowledge irrespective of their interactional experience (Brown 1987: 215). What should be noted is that it is essential to have knowledge about how communication context varies culturally, and that it is also important to remember that culture contexts are neither right nor wrong, neither better nor worse, they are just different. Therefore, in intercultural communication, "context is a form of cultural adaptation to a particular setting or environment".

According to Thomas, the types of information conveyed include two levels. At level 1, there exists the attitude of the speaker towards the information. At level 2, two elements are included, namely, ①the speech act or communicative intent of the utterance; ②attitude of the speaker towards the hearer. In the process of communication, as one moves from level 2 ① to ②, one is moving from the pragmalinguistic to the sociopragmatic end of the continuum and at the same time from what is language – specific to what is culture-specific .

4.1.2　The Analysis of Pragmalinguistic Failures

Pragmalinguistic failure is simply a question of highly conventionalized usage which can be taught straightforwardly as part of grammar. It occurs when the pragmatic force, or meaning, which is assigned by speakers to an utterance, differs from the meaning that native speakers usually assign to it. If we put it in another way, it occurs when speech act strategies are inappropriately transferred from the first language to the second language.

The most common pragmalinguistic failure generally falls into six groups:

(1)Equating Chinese lexical expressions with English expressions.

a. A Chinese student asks a native English speaker to take a picture for her and her friend. After her instructions on how to operate the camera, the native speaker checks and asks:

English speaker: Shall I just push the button?

Chinese student: Of course.

The English speaker first sends out an inquiry, which requires some confirmed information. The Chinese student intends to give an affirmative reply. Unfortunately, he misuses"of course". In the light of the response of the Chinese student, the pragmatic force of "of course" differs from the native speaker's. The Chinese student intends to agree by using "of course", meaning "certainly, exactly, or you are right". But in fact, "of course" in that context carries an accusatory meaning to native speakers, which implies "it is so easy and simple that only a fool may ask such a question!" This explains why the native speaker is so annoyed at her answer.

b. In a Chinese restaurant, an American customer talks with a waitress.

Customer: I'd like to have a steak, followed by roast duck and potatoes, please.

Waitress：What?

The waitress uses the Chinese way of expression"what" to ask for the repetition of the customer's order, but "what" sounds like a stiff reply rather than a polite request. So the correct expression should be "I beg your pardon?" or "Pardon me?"

（2）Violating the way of expression of English native speakers and misusing some other expressions.

a. A Chinese teacher, Ms. Wang, taught a group of English students Chinese at a Chinese university. When she finished one section, she said, "So much for Lesson 2. Now let's look at the exercises."

After hearing this remark, the English students felt quite funny in that situation. In this case, when the teacher Ms. Wang said"So much for Lesson 2", she might mean "that's all for lesson 2" or "we have finished the text of lesson 2." However, she is not aware that "so much for ..." carries a negative or derogatory sense to a native speaker, which means some kind of dismissal, that is, "Thank goodness! That's over!"

b. A foreign manager in a joint-venture company speaks highly of the Chinese secretary's performance.

Manager：Thanks a lot. That's a great help.

Secretary：Never mind.

The Chinese secretary means to express"不用谢"or "没关系". But she doesn't make it clear that "Never mind" is used when the opposite party makes an apology to some one and he doesn't take it seriously at the same time. This is just a kind of polite formula used to comfort others. It is better to say, "It's my pleasure."

（3）Using the expressive structure of Chinese language indiscriminately in English expressions.

a. An American went shopping in a department.

Chinese sales girl：What do you want?

American：（embarrassed）

The Chinese girl wants to say"你要点儿什么?" to greet the American.

But in the light of the American way, she ought to say, "Can I help you?" on such an occasion.

b. A tourist guide leads a group of Americans to visit a museum in Xi' an. On their way to the museum, they are informed that this visit has to be called off because of the interior decorations. They are very disappointed and ask the guide:

Tourist: So you didn't know that beforehand, did you?

Guide: Yes.

Tourist: You didn't mean that you knew it in advance, did you?

Guide: Yes, Miss.

In this conversation, the Chinese tourist guide confuses the Chinese way with the English way in answering the disjunctive questions. When he answers"yes", what he means is "Yes, I knew that beforehand.", which is against his real intent "I didn't know that beforehand." As a matter of fact, the guide should reply in this way "No, I didn't." to the disjunctive question according to the English way.

(4)Only understanding the literal meaning rather than the real intention of the speaker.

a. In the classroom.

Teacher: Can you work out this problem?

Student: Yes.

In English, "Can you ..." is a highly conventionalized form of politeness, which is likely to be interpreted by native speakers as a request to do something, rather than a question as to one's ability to do something. The teacher intends to call on the student to work out the problem in the text, but the student only interprets it as a kind of question concerning his ability. Therefore, the teacher must be bewildered by the student's reply.

b. In the classroom.

Teacher: Would you like to read the text?

Student: No, I wouldn't.

Generally, the native speakers predictably assign certain pragmatic force to certain utterances. So the utterance "Would you like to …" is a highly conventionalized polite request or directive in an English classroom. But the student's reply sounds too rude and direct. He merely views the utterance as a general and common question, not realizing that it carries a sense of strong politeness.

(5) Misusing complete sentences and ignoring the particular implication that they produce in some special circumstances.

a. In the nursery.

A: Have you brought your coat?

B: Yes, I have brought my coat.

According to Leech, complete sentence responses violate the textual pragmatic "principle of economy" and it is easy to see how they can create an unfortunate impression. B's reply sounds petulant or positively testy. From the pragmatic point of view, B violates the maxim of quantity of the cooperative principle so that A may draw an inference which doesn't exist in B's utterance.

Some teaching techniques may actually increase the likelihood of such a pragmatic failure. Such a pragmatic failure may attribute to teaching materials (inappropriate use of modality), classroom practice and some other teaching-induced errors.

b. In a classroom, the teacher asks a student.

Teacher: Can you hear clearly?

Student: Yes, I can hear clearly.

This conversation also shows that the student misuses the complete sentence structure. It sounds impatient and mechanical. It is better to say, "Yes, I can."

(6) Neglecting to use different expressions on differentoccasions.

a. A and B are good friends. A asks for help from B. A says: "Could you possibly help me with the table?" A's tone sounds a little bit strange. It's unnecessary to have indirectness and understatement among friends' interaction. Therefore, the expression "Help me with the table" is all right.

b. At the library.

Professor: When shall I return this book?

Librarian: Perhaps you could read through this by Friday.

In English, the expressions are not always pragmatically interchangeable. Thus, it might be acceptable and suitable to say to one's inferior "Perhaps you could read through this by Friday." However, it might be more polite to say to one's superior "Could you possibly read through this by Friday?" Native speakers would interpret "Perhaps you could" as impositive rather than a request and as either somewhat authoritarian or else sarcastic. This is a kind of pragmatic overgeneralization of target language (L2).

In a word, the inappropriate transference of speech act strategies from L1 to L2 is a frequent cause of pragmalinguistic failures. It is evident that the foreign learner is not noticeably more sensitive about having pragmalinguistic failures than about having grammatical mistakes corrected. I don't think the above six types of pragmalinguistic failures are adequate. In fact, in the process of intercultural communication, there are much more sources of such pragmatic failures than we expect. In communicating with a person from a different culture, we ought to keep in mind that speech act strategies of the source language (L1) should not be transferred directly to the target language (L2). L1 interference should be avoided as much as possible.

4.1.3   The Analysis on the Sociopragmatic Failures

Sociopragmatic failures stem from cross-culturally different perceptions of what constitutes appropriate linguistic behavior. Compared with pragmalinguistic failures, it is much more difficult to deal with, since it involves the speakers' system of beliefs, desires, intentions as much as their knowledge of language. In fact, interaction between native speakers and non-native speakers readily exhibits how the lack of shared linguistic systems can result in the failure in communication. The differences of regions, ethnicity, politics and social class are undoubtedly reflected as much by a diversity of pragmatic norms as by linguistic variations.

Sociopragmatic failures occur when social conditions placed on language in use are different. It has been well proved that speech communities differ in their assessment of speakers' and hearers' social distance and social power, their rights and their obligations, and the degree of imposition involved in particular communicative acts.

Pragmatic expectations andassessments are indeed culture-specific. It is likely that a foreign speaker will assess size of imposition, social-distance, etc. differently from a native speaker. Thomas suggests that: It is cross-culturally mismatches in the assessment of social distance, of what makes up an imposition, of when an attempt at a "face-threatening act" should be abandoned, and in evaluating relative power, rights, and obligations, etc., which cause sociopragmatic failure.

In the process of intercultural communication, the culturally unwarranted response is linked in part to low linguistic competence and in part to low social cultural knowledge. Differential knowledge of culturally appropriate ways of responding can lead to sociopragmatic failures too.

Illustrations of sociopragmatic failures that stem from cross-culturally different assessments are countless and enormous. Here, I just pick out some to analyze the pragmatic failures from the sociopragmatic point of view.

(1)Sociopragmatic failures caused by ignorance of contextual factors in intercultural communication.

Context is a dynamic, not a static concept. It is to be understood as the continually changing surroundings, in the widest sense, that enable the participants in the communication process to interact, and in which the linguistic expressions of their interaction become intelligible. Using language tactfully in communication involves choosing different language forms in the light of different occasions, different interactors.

a. Wang shared an apartment with other students. One day, the landlord came to the house to collect her and other tenants' rents and chatted with Wang for a while. When all the rents were paid, the landlord rose to leave. Wang said, "Would you like to stay a bit longer?" The landlord seemed unprepared for this "invitation", he paused, then said, "No, I have some thing else to do. I am on my way to hospital."

In this story, Wang's remark "Would you like to stay a bit longer?" is taken as an unexpected invitation by the native speaker of English, the landlord. This invitation sounds noticeably odd in that context because Wang doesn't take into account the contextual variables of social distance and the power relationship. If it is in the context of Chinese cultural background, then Wang's invitation would sound reasonable and polite. In the context of American cultural background, however, it sounds too abrupt and makes the other feel uneasy and out of place. In English, when the power relationship is involved in the communication, as when the landlord is collecting the rent from the tenants, an acceptable greeting for the tenants is "Good bye, see you later."

However, supposing in the situation where a policeman helped an inhabitant with his lost deposit. When the policeman brought the money back to him, and was to leave from his house, the inhabitant could say: "Would you like a cup of coffee before you go?" or something like "Thank you very much. Good bye!" The difference here is that in the first case the landlord is coming for his own sake (to collect the rent), while in the second one the policeman is doing somebody a favor.

b. An American professor said to his students in the English class, "Before I start my lecture, I would like to give you a test in order to know where you are." After hearing this, many students were a little bit puzzled, they asked, "Why, Professor, we are in the classroom."

If we analyze this conversation from the specific context, apparently the students commit a kind of sociopragmatic failure. They only figured out the literal meaning or the natural meaning in the general situation (The professor wants to know which place they are in). But they didn't sense the implied meaning or the speaker-meaning (The professor wants to know the students' present level in English reading). If any of the two interactors doesn't understand the contextual cues, he or she will not give a relevant answer to the question.

Language communication is a complex activity. Only when the interactors of different cultures share the common knowledge of the context can they achieve the goal of communication. Otherwise, misunderstanding will occur.

(2) Sociopragmatic failures caused by different perspectives of cultural values.

If we say that pragmalinguistic failures are at the surface level, then I should say sociopragmatic failures are at the deep level. Most of the sociopragmatic failures are due to the different concepts of cultural values.

The most difficult type of pragmatic failures occurs when pragmatic principles, such as the politeness principle conflict with other deeply held values such as truthfulness or sincerity.

Leech says: But on thing that cannot be denied is that pragmatic principles introduce communicative values, such as truthfulness, into the study of language. Traditionally, linguists have avoided referring to such values, feeling that they undermine one's claim for objectivity. But so long as the values we consider are the ones we suppose, on empirical grounds, to be operative in society, rather than the ones we impose on society, then there is no reason to exclude them from our enquiry.

Cultural values are the basis for our actions. They guide our behavior and help us determine what is right and what is wrong; what is good and what is bad. Value systems are culturally diverse, and they determine differences of communicative acts among different cultures.

a. A Chinese policeman goes to his British superior and asks for leave to take his mother to hospital. Here is the conversation:

Chinese policeman: Sir?

British superior: Yes, what is it?

Chinese policeman: My mother is not very well, Sir.

British superior: So?

Chinese policeman: She has to go into hospital, Sir.

British superior: Well, get on with it. What do you want?

Chinese policeman: On Thursday, Sir.

British superior: Bloody hell, man. What do you want?

Chinese policeman: Nothing, Sir.

Most Chinese comment that the British officer has no human feelings. On the other hand, the comment of the native speakers of English is that the Chinese policeman is a terrible guy, and he is not frank enough. The cause of this pragmatic failure is obvious. The Chinese policeman wants to ask for a leave because of his mother's illness. As a superior, the officer should have shown his care for the policeman and granted him a leave of absence according to the Chinese culture. However, in the English culture, there is the fact that whether a person's mother is ill or not has nothing to do with the other. What the British officer is anxious to know is that what the Chinese policeman wants from him. In a word, different cultural value lends to this pragmatic failure.

Many speech acts which are considered rude and impolite by people from other cultures are actually taken for granted and considered appropriate and decent in the native cultures because these have been conventionalized in the said cultures. The actual difficulty in intercultural communication is cultural misunderstandings. For instance, it is polite and natural to complete an offer or invitation and response in a single act (direct "yes" or "no" response) in the English culture but it is also polite to deal with it by a series of acts in the Chinese culture. It is natural to the Chinese when an offer or invitation is made once, then refused, and so on and so forth.

Since feelings or actions that are considered morally good or socially useful in some cultures might turn out to be bad or useless in others, words and expressions used to describe certain actions would have differing affective meaning. Some direct comments or questions about certain personal matters are appropriate and friendly in the Chinese culture but unacceptable or ever offensive in the English culture. One example is that a Chinese might say to his or her friend,"Oh，your dress is much more expensive than the one I bought the other day. It is not worth that much." Such comment is friendly among the Chinese people but seem to make a native English person feel inferior to someone else and thus very offensive.

Another example is that a Chinese can say to a longtime departed friend,"你还是老样子，一点也没变。"Suppose this Chinese speaks to an American friend, "Hello, haven't seen you for ages! You haven't changed at all!" This will surely offend a native speaker of English by implicating that he or she lacks some change or makes no progress. The truth of the American culture lies in "change". In American's eyes, "change" embodies the spirit of breaking with convention and innovation. "Change" means "developing" and "progress". As for the Chinese people, they advocate "steady" and seek progress and development in "steady". This conception of cultural value is far different from Americans' value of adventure and enterprising.

Some topics which people enjoy discussing in one culture are the ones people attempt to avoid in the other culture: what people are usually concerned with probably cause offence to the privacy in the other culture. In the Chinese culture, such topics as income, religion belief, marital status are free topics and there are no limitations on them. But the similar topics evidently pose threat to the personal privacy in the English culture. In a word, sociolinguistic failures are owing to cultural differences. The following example is used to strengthen this idea.

b. A：Here is some little thing for you，but it's not very good.

B：No, no. I really can't accept.

A：But you must. It was bought specially for you.

B：No, no, no, I can't ... I won't take it.

A：Oh，come on, take it.

B：(taking it slowly) oh, all right, you really shouldn't have gone to the expense.

In this case, A is an American. He bought a gift for his Chinese friend. He is not satisfied with B's response, for the latter has not realized the different attitudes toward receiving gifts. According to the English culture, when a person is given a gift, he is inclined to unfold the package and take a look, which indicates the receiver's respect for the giver. In the Chinese culture, it is not polite to open the gift box. Perhaps the gift might not be valuable, so unfolding the package of gift on the spot may make him lose face.

Quite a number of cross-cultural conflict of values may be shown in the "deep structure of pragmatic failures—sociopragmatic failures". In addition to the previously mentioned instances, we often see the examples of Americans using expressions such as "We really must get together sometime." For an American, they are simply polite, meaningless words, but the non-American often interprets it as genuine invitation and is hurt to find later that it was not intended as such. It's only a causal remark. The non-Americans thus identify "insincerity" on the part of Americans and it is regarded as a source of considerable irritation and frustration to non-Americans. If such an expression is marked by some mention of time, place, or activity, then it may be taken as a "genuine" invitation.

In sum, pragmalinguistic failures and sociolinguistic failures co-exist in the process of intercultural communication, with the former being the surface structure of miscommunication and the latter being the deep structure. The first is language-specific and the teachers are responsible for correcting them. The second is culture-specific, which is a reflection of students' systems of values and beliefs. It is hard to correct them other than introducing some means to cultivate the students' cultural awareness. Being EFL teachers and students, they must concern themselves with investigating their causes and doing something to avoid them.

4.2　Underlying Causes of Pragmatic Failures

After some analysis of instances, I think the causes of pragmatic failures lie in the following aspects.

In the first place, L2 learners do not always transfer some aspects of universal or first language-based pragmatic knowledge to second language communication. They tend to understand utterances at their face value, rather than infer the underlying meaning. They usually do not take advantage of context information. In the first language situation, some evidences show that L2 learners are often quite sensitive to context in choosing pragmatic strategies. Nevertheless, they may not well differentiate such context variables as social distance and power in second language situation.

For example, an English person may say, "I am sorry I can't stay long." "Thank you for a wonderful evening." or "It was nice seeing you." when he is about to depart. In responding to this, many Chinese would like to translate literally the Chinese greeting formula "Would you like to stay a bit longer?"(不多坐一会儿吗?) without considering the contextual factors. In two friends' meeting, when one notices the other is in low spirit and is about to leave, the first one could say, "Never mind, you could stay a bit longer." If their social distance is very near and there is not power relationship involved, the host could say, "Come again when you have time." But when there is power relationship involved, saying "Would you like to stay a bit longer?" when they plan to leave would cause them to think "for what?"

Secondly, the failures can also be caused by the negative transfer of pragmatic knowledge from the first language. This is manifested in two aspects. The inappropriate transfer can occur at the pragmalingistic level. This happens when speakers try to transfer from their first language to utterances of the second language, which are semantically or syntactically equivalent, but due to different interpretive bias, it will carry a different pragmatic force in the target language. The misuse of "of course" in the previous example is just within this category.

On the other hand, the negative transfer can be at the sociopragmatic level. It has been argued that the sociopragmatic failure is caused by the mismatches in the intercultural communication in terms of social distance, power relationship, conceptions of social values. These mismatches affect linguistic choices in turn. A non-native speaker may judge relative power or social distance in a way different from that of a native speaker. These differences are most clearly demonstrated in the communication between teachers and students from two different cultures. In the students' own culture, teachers may have a higher status than they are in the English cultural background. This social judgment causes the students to behave more deferentially than would normally be expected. For example, in the western countries, it is believed that teachers and students are peers. There isn't so much social distance and relative power involved in their relationship. That's why American students dare to challenge the teachers' authority. They may use some direct questions or expressions against the teachers. In the Chinese culture, teachers are highly respected. A Chinese saying "a teacher for a day is a father for a lifetime" demonstrates this tenet very well. Many Chinese students are scared to challenge the teachers' authority, even if they feel puzzled about the teachers' ideas. For instance, after an English class is over, a Chinese student says to the American teacher, "Mr. Grey, you've made a wonderful lecture!" The Chinese student is against the maxim of quality and makes others feel that he is boasting and flattering and appears somewhat hypocritical.

Thirdly, pragmatic failures can be caused by factors related to teaching. It has been argued that there is a lack of authenticity in both the teaching materials used and the classroom discourse, especially so in the EFL contexts. At present, overemphasis on metalinguistic knowledge can suggest that there is a one-to-one correlation between a certain grammatical category and a speech act. In the example "So much for page 10", the pragmatic failure is mainly caused by the inauthentic input in the classroom teaching. It can also be that learners are only taught the linguistic form and are not aware of the pragmatic force carried in them. Teachers seldom add pragmatic knowledge to the teaching of English grammar in practice. Take the teaching of "to be + inf." for instance. Teachers should not only tell the students some usages of this structure, they should also tell the students that this structure usually goes together with the second person subject, indicating that the relationship between the speaker and the hearer is superior-inferior. Its purpose is to send out an order as in this sentence "You're to be here by eight."

4.3 Test of Pragmatic Competence

4.3.1 Purpose of the Test

Ever since 1972 when American sociolinguist Dell Hymes published his book entitled *On Communicative Competence*, people have begun to focus on the aspect of language application in various contexts. Many foreign language teachers also become aware of the importance of development of communicative competence. In the process of intercultural communication, studying the obstacles in communication has become more and more significant to foreign language teaching. In the last two decades, a number of experts in the field of foreign language teaching and research have achieved some results with regard to English-Chinese pragmatic differences, such as Hu Wenzhong, Deng Yanchang and Liu Runqing, He Ziran and Yan Zhuang, Wang Dexing, Hong Gang. But there are few people dealing with the task of pragmatic failures in relation to non-English majors' grammatical competence and pragmatic competence.

Owing to the increasing rate of pragmatic failures in the process of intercultural communication, a test concerning the failures in intercultural communication is carried out. The results of testees' performance are analyzed and illustrated by virtue of some pragmatic theories. I want to find out: ① In what areas and aspects the testees tend to commit pragmatic errors. ② Whether the students with greater linguistic ability have greater pragmatic ability. In other words, whether a student's linguistic ability is in direct ratio with his pragmatic ability. ③ Exploring the implications to EFL learning and teaching by studying the pragmatic failures and discussing the effective strategies to avoid pragmatic failures in the process of intercultural communication by the Chinese EFL students.

4.3.2 Theoretical Grounds

This test is designed to explore the relationship between students' linguistic competence and their pragmatic competence. Competence includes grammatical competence and communicative competence. Grammatical competence gained popularity through the work of Chomsky and then was interpreted as the exclusive aim of language teaching and learning. It is discovered that language is constrained by many social and cultural factors and learning a language involves more than memorizing rules and words. The concept of communicative competence has evolved to complement grammatical competence. Grammatical competence refers to the language system and communicative competence refers to language use. Broadly speaking, communicative competence is highlighted in the process of intercultural communication and it functions as much as the pragmatic competence. In this sense, we may equate communicative competence with pragmatic competence.

In conducting the survey, I adopt Jenny Thomas's idea that pragmatic failures fall into two categories: pragmalinguistic failures and sociolinguistic failures. All the questions are selected and arranged on the basis of these theoretical grounds.

4.3.3 Method

The participants in this study were second-year college students of science and engineering from two classes and post-graduates in Xi' an University of Technology. There are 26 post-graduates and 30 students in class A with higher English proficiency level and 29 students in class B with comparatively lower English proficiency level. The students of class A come from the Department of Management. The students of class B are from the Department of Hydroelectricity. They are given a proficiency test before they are chosen as the subjects in this experiment(see Table 4.1).

Table 4.1　Statistics of English Proficiency Test

Subjects	Score of each item				
	Listening	Reading	Vocabulary	Cloze	Mean
Post-graduates	15.6	34.2	15.2	16.2	81.2
Class A	14.4	30.5	13.4	14	72.3
Class B	13.7	28.7	11.3	14.8	68.5

The mean score of post-graduates is 81.2. The mean score of class A is 72.3 and the mean score of class B is 68.5(the total score is 100). From Table 4.1 we can see that the post-graduates' grammatical competence ranks in the first place, whereas class B's grammatical competence ranks in the last place, class A's grammatical competence is at the intermediate level. These three groups are chosen as samples in the survey from which the author wants to know whether the students with better linguistic competence have better pragmatic competence in the test, whether the students who are more competent in language expression make fewer pragmatic errors in the course of intercultural communication.

The test for pragmatic competence contains 20 multiple-choice questions, which fall into two groups. The first group is mainly about pragmalinguistic questions, ranging from question 1 – 10. The second group covers sociopragmatic questions, which are from question 11 – 20. Pragmalinguistic questions are used to exam two aspects of abilities. One is the ability to understand the pragmatic implication of certain utterance. The other is the ability to express one's own intention or understand other's intention in specific context. Sociopragmatic questions are largely used to test students' ability to make use of language expressions appropriately in light of interactors' different cultural backgrounds and different social contexts.

The questions in the test are collected and edited from the following channels: ① Some questions are from the *listening course of College English* published by Shanghai Foreign Language Education Press; ② The author's personal teaching experience in these years; ③ Some teachers from the author's department also offer some questions. ④ A few questions are selected from He Ziran and Yan Zhuang's survey.

This test is held on three different days. The students are told that they can finish the test within 30 minutes. They may refer to the dictionary if they meet strange and difficult words so that they may avoid some pragmatic failures caused by the difficulty in understanding grammatical and semantic matters.

4.3.4 Results and Analysis(see Table 4.2 and Table 4.3)

Table 4.2 Distribution of Score in the Test for Pragmatic Competence

Subjects	Rate of each score				
	<50	$50-59$	$60-69$	$70-79$	$80-89$
Post-graduates	5/26	7/26	10/26	3/26	1/26
Class A	1/30	7/30	8/30	9/30	5/30
Class B	6/29	8/29	12/29	3/29	0/29

Table 4.3 Scores of Subjects at Three Levels

Subjects	Post-graduates	Class A	Class B
Top score	80	95	80
Lowest score	50	60	55
Mean score	62.3	75.3	62.1

The results are presented in the above two tables. In Table 4.2, we can see that under the range of 59 points, there are 12 out of the 26 students in post-graduates. There are 8 out of the 30 students in class A. Still there are 14 out of the 29 students in class B. In other words, the rate of failing is respectively 46%, 27% and 48%. What is more, in the range of over 60 points, there are 14 students in post-graduates; 22 students in class A; 15 students in class B. This demonstrates that the passing rate is respectively 54%, 73% and 52%. In the range from 70 points to 89 points, there are 4 students from post-graduates, 14 students from class A and 3 students from class B, whose percentage is 15%, 47% and 10% respectively.

We can reach some conclusions from Table 4.2. First, we find out that the students from class A make the best performance. Second, in comparison with students of class B, the post-graduates do not achieve the better results. In other words, there is hardly any significant difference between the two groups in the matter of pragmatic performance. Thirdly, this indicates that pragmatic competence among the three groups of subjects is not in agreement with their respective linguistic competence.

Table 4.2 also shows that the students of class A make the best performance in the test, whereas the post-graduates make the relatively poorer performance even though their grammatical competence is regarded as the best among the three groups of students. According to my investigation, more than 50% of the post-graduates continue the advanced study after they graduated from the university for 2 to 5 years. They don't have so much energy, time and chance to acquire the intercultural and pragmatic knowledge. The students of class A and class B stay on the campus for much longer time and they understand more cultural knowledge and pragmatic principles. One exception is that the students of class B mainly come from the remote and mountain areas. They don't stand out both in the grammatical competence and pragmatic competence. But we can see that the discrepancy between the post-graduates' pragmatic competence and theirs is not so striking.

Table 4.3 demonstrates that the students from class A achieve the top score, whereas one of the post-graduates gets the lowest score, which is a little bit surprising. The mean scores might indicate that the post-graduates performance is almost as poor as the students of class B.

Table 4.4 illustrates the failure rate of the 20 questions finished by the three groups of students. From this table, we may observe that firstly, the students' performance of the three groups is far from satisfactory. Secondly, out of the 85 testees, no one achieves the full score. Generally speaking, the difference of the failure rate of the three groups concerning the 20 questions is not so remarkable. Thirdly, the three groups have almost the common tendency toward some respects of pragmatic failure. Lastly, the average failure rate about these questions is different, with class A students' being the lowest and post-graduates' being the highest. At the same time, the post-graduates' failure rate is almost the same as class B students', which is a little bit surprising.

Questions 1 – 10 are concerning pragmatic matter of language itself. In question 5, the situation is: an American lady stepped on a Chinese youngster and apologized, "I am terribly sorry." The students are asked to give a proper reply to her apology. Of the 85 students, 64 students (75%) choose "It doesn't matter." Only 5 students (6%) choose "That's all right." as the reply. In question 8, an American said to a Chinese partner, "That's very kind of you." 62 students (more than 70% of the total students) choose "Never mind." as the reply. The English "Never mind." and the Chinese "没关系" have similar literal meanings but they have different pragmatic functions and are used on different occasions. In Chinese, "没关系" can be used as a reply to both the "appreciation" and "apology" of the opposite side. For example, "太感谢你了!" – "没关系" or "实在对不起" – "没关系" In English, "Never mind" can only be used as a reply to "apology". The results of the survey show that the errors that students tend to make most lie in the usage of some fixed expressions, in particular, some expressions which exist in both Chinese and English and meanwhile have similar literal meanings.

Table 4.4　Failure Rate of 20 Questions among the Three Groups

Number	Failure rate of each subject		
	Post-graduates	Class A	Class B
1	46%	43%	41%
2	55%	42%	51%
3	33%	39%	43%
4	34%	32%	41%
5	55%	47%	46%
6	43%	51%	53%
7	45%	42%	52%
8	63%	62%	67%
9	51%	49%	51%
10	45%	38%	40%
11	54%	57%	61%
12	39%	35%	32%
13	45%	35%	37%
14	38%	29%	35%
15	29%	32%	27%
16	40%	35%	36%
17	50%	41%	43%
18	34%	28%	33%
19	41%	28%	34%
20	57%	55%	52%
Average	45%	41%	44%

Questions 11 – 20 are about sociopragmatic failures. In general, sociopragmatic failure is essentially caused by discrepancy between the

Chinese culture and the English culture. Take question 11 of the test for example. An American customer wants to buy some "Longjing" tea, but the tea has been sold out. The dialogue goes as follows.

Customer: Do you have Longjing tea?

Salesgirl: Oh, no, we run out.

Customer: Oaky, thanks anyway.

Salesgirl: …

As regards to the reply, as many as 75% students choose "You are welcome", which is equivalent to the Chinese "不用谢". In China, customers are accustomed to showing their appreciation for the service. By contrast, in Western countries shop assistants should thank customers for their visit and when they can't offer some service to the customers, they should express their apology. So the salesgirl should say "I am sorry".

From Table 4.4, we may see that the failure rate about question 20 is very high. As for the post-graduates, class A students and class B students, thefailure rate is respectively 57%, 55% and 52%. The context is: on the way to a clothing show, the wife of an English manager is talking with a secretary. When the wife says, "It's really cold tonight", most of the students think that the secretary should say, "Here, take my jacket", which is not correct. The reason is that the students don't know "It's really cold tonight" is in fact a kind of exchange of greetings rather than a request for clothes among friends in the American culture. So here the students violate the principle of politeness.

From all the findings of the test, we should point out that some pragmalinguistic failures and some sociopragmatic failures caused by some different politeness principles in different cultures are not so hard to overcome. We may regard them as pragmatic failures at the surface structure. On the other hand, it is very hard to overcome some sociopragmatic failures which originate from the level of deep cultural psychology, for example, foreigners' compliments to the Chinese. Because the concept of "modesty" has been deeply rooted in Chinese's mind, even if they know how to react to the foreigners' compliment, they are used to refusing compliments. This is due to the difference in the deep cultural psychology of the English people and the Chinese people.

In conclusion, in combination with the four tables, we can see that the post-graduates might have a good command of grammar and vocabulary, or linguistic competence, but their cultural knowledge may not be correspondingly rich and sound, which accordingly leads to their poor pragmatic competence. There is not a striking difference between the performance of post-graduates and class B students in the matter of pragmatic competence, though the linguistic competence of these two groups are at different levels. This shows that high level of grammatical competence does not guarantee concomitant high level of pragmatic competence.

The results of the survey strengthens my idea that much input of linguistic knowledge does not necessarily leads to the corresponding improvement of language application and pragmatic competence. Because of the lack of pragmatic ability, pragmalinguistic failures and sociolinguistic failures are caused by the testees.

4.4　A Questionnaire Concerning Aspects of Pragmatic Competence and Pragmatic Failures

The purpose of designing this part is to get the feedback from the subjects about their attitudes towards the importance of the cultivation of pragmatic competence and to see how they respond to the question of pragmatic failures in the process of intercultural communication. 15 students of class A and 15 students of class B from Xi'an University of Technology are chosen as the subjects.

The questionnaire is composed of 8 questions. The first 7 are generally YES-NO questions which mainly focus on some aspects of pragmatic failures and the students' ideas abut pragmatic competence. The last is a short-answer question. The answers from the subjects are generally consistent with what Ⅱ have assumed(see Table 4.5).

Table 4.5   Result of Questionnaire

Number	Precentage of each class	
	Class A	Class B
1	53％— NO	73％— NO
2	67％— pragmatic errors	73％— pragmatic errors
3	60％— NO	67％— NO
4	80％— linguistic competence	60％— linguistic competence
5	60％— NO	67％— NO
6	87％— test	87％— test
7	80％— NO	87％— NO

From Table 4.5, we can see something interesting. To be specific, as for the first question, 8 students of class A (53％) and 11 students of class B (73％) choose NO. When the students are asked what makes them more uneasy when they are communicating with an American, 10 students of class A (67％) and 11 students of class B (73％) choose pragmatic errors. This shows that students have already felt that pragmatic errors are more serious than grammatical errors in communication. Also, in question 3, 9 students of class A (60％) and 10 students of class B (67％) say NO, which suggests that the students are not satisfied with the present teaching methodology. As for question 4, 12 students of class A (80％) and 9 students of class B (60％) think that linguistic competence is more important than pragmatic competence in English study. Later on, I discussed with them. Many students said that a good command of linguistic ability would lead them to the higher grades in the CET-4/6 examinations. As for question 5, 9 students of class A (60％) and 10 students of class B (67％) think they seldom read some English books to enlarge their cultural knowledge. In answering question 6, 13 students of both class A and class B (87％) agree that the present CET-4/6 testing system makes them ignore the cultivation of pragmatic competence. This shows that the present language testing system should be reformed to direct the students to the right way of language learning. For question 7, 12 students of class A (80%) and 13 students of class B (87%) choose NO. This means that teachers rarely impart pragmatic knowledge in class. The reason is partially on the present EFL teaching system, partially on the teachers' own lack of competence.

As for the last question, all the students answer that teachers should focus on the cultivation of students' pragmatic competence without neglecting the training of students' grammatical competence at the same time. They expect teachers to teach them some pragmatic strategies to avoid pragmatic failures. They also expect to be offered more chances to communicate with foreigners and they think that cultural knowledge should be offered in the process of language teaching.

From this survey, it may be concluded that students' attitude towards pragmatic failures and pragmatic competence is positive. But unfortunately, because of the present language testing system, which is grades-oriented, and the teaching methodology, students have to spend much time on the strengthening of their linguistic competence and tend to ignore the cultivation of their pragmatic competence. That is the main reason why pragmatic failures become so common among the EFL learners in recent years.

第4章 跨文化交际中的语用失误

语用问题中涉及很多语域问题。然而,从不同文化的交际过程中遇到的问题来看,与语用失误相关的是人们交际的具体方法和相应的理解方式。为了分析语用失效,我们应该更好地理解什么是社会文化知识,什么是超文化知识,以及暴露在人们交际行为当中的世界观和价值观。

4.1 语用失误的类型

Miller 提出,我们大多数时候对他人的误解并不是因为听不懂他们所说的话,或无法分析他们所说的句子。不同文化的交流难点在于我们常常误解了说话者的意图。Jenny Thomas(1983)把"语用失误"这一专业术语定义为"无法理解话语的意图"。

语用失误是指跨文化交际中出现的失败。Thomas 选择了"语用失误"("pragmatic failute")这个术语表达,而非"语用错误"("pragmatic error"),因为它不像语言性错误一样可以通过制定严密的语法规则来避免或纠正,语用能力所包含的远不止明确的规则。因此,不能说一段话语的语用用意(pragmatic force)或意义(meaning)是"错误"的,只能说它没有达到说话者的目的。跨文化语用失误分为两种类型:语言语用失误和社交语用失误。

4.1.1 区别语言语用失误和社交语用失误的必要性

语言语用失误基本可以看作是语言问题,是由语用用意中语言编码的不同而造成的;而社交语用失误则是由适宜的语言行为构成的跨文化感知差异引起的。为了按照说话者的意愿解释一段话的用意,听者必须考虑到语境和语言暗示。语境往往能够单独决定一段话语中所包含的用意。事实上,每种文化中,一段话语的语内表现行为的暗含之意依赖于某些特殊的语境,因此,任何话语只有在相关的语境暗示前提下才有具体确切的意义,而且其中的语境暗示是说话者和听话者的文化知识或经验中所共有的,或是听话者的行为中提到了与理解话语有关的信息,无论是说话者-听话者经历中先前存在的,还是与双方的互动经历无关的共有知识。要注意的是,交流语境因文化的不同而不同,这一点很关键,另外还有一点也非常重要,文化语境没有正确错误之分,也没有优劣之分,只有不同的区别。因此,在跨文化交流中,"语境是适应某一特定文化背景或文化环境的一种形式"。

　　Thomas 认为,信息传达的类型包括两个层面。第一层面上存在着说话者对于信息的态度。第二层面包括两个元素,即,①话语中的言语行为或交际意图;②说话者对于听者的态度。交际过程中,第二层面的①过渡至②意味着从这一连续体的语用语言学端向社会语用学端的过渡,同时也是从特定语言向特定文化的过渡。

4.1.2　语言语用失误的分析

　　语言语用失误是一个高度惯例化用法的简单问题,可以简单地作为语法的一部分进行学习。当说话者赋予一段话语的语用用意或意义与母语使用者为这段话语赋予的意义存在区别时,便会发生语言语用失效。换句话说,当第一语言到第二语言的言语行为策略转换存在不当时,便会发生语言语用失效。

　　最常见的语言语用失效一般来说分为六类:

　　(1)将中文词汇表达与英文表达等同起来。

　　a. 一位中国学生请一位母语为英语的人士为她和她的朋友拍一张照片。在她向对方介绍了如何操作相机之后,说母语者看过之后问到:

　　English speaker:Shall I just push the button?

　　Chinese student:Of course.

　　英语为母语者首先提出了一个问题,需要得到确定的答案。中国学生也想给出确定的答案。不幸的是,她用错了"of course"这个词。根据中国学生的回答,"of course"的语用用意与母语使用者存在不同。中国学生想要通过"of course"这个词对对方的说法表示赞同,意思是"certainly,exactly,or you are right"。事实上,在这一语境中,"of course"对于母语使用者来说有一定的指责意味,意思是"it is so easy and simple that only a fool may ask such a question!"这也解释了为什么母语使用者会对她的回答感到恼怒。

b. 在一家中国餐厅,美国客人在和侍者交谈。

Customer：I'd like to have a steak, followed by roast duck and potatoes, please.

Waitress：What?

侍者所说的"what"是中文方式的表达,是想让客人再重复一遍他点的菜,但是"what"听起来更像是一个僵硬的反应而非礼貌的请求。因此,正确的表达方式应该是"I beg your pardon?"或者"Pardon me?"

(2)违反英语为母语者的表达方式或误用其他表达。

a. 在中国的一所大学里,一位中国老师,王女士,正在给一班英国学生上中文课。在结束了一节内容之后,她说,"So much for Lesson 2. Now let's look at the exercises."

对于英国学生来说,这种情境下说这番话语会显得非常滑稽。在这种情况下,当王老师说"So much for Lesson 2"时,她的意思可能是"that's all for lesson 2"或"we have finished the text of lesson 2."然而,她没有意识到的是,"so much for..."这种表达方式对于母语使用者来说带有一定的负面或贬低意味,有一点解散的意思,即"Thank goodness! That's over!"

b. 一家合资公司的外籍经理对中国秘书的表现赞赏有加。

Manager：Thanks a lot. That's a great help.

Secretary：Never mind.

中国秘书想要表达的意思是"不用谢"或者"没关系"。但是她并没有表达清楚这个意思,"Never mind"通常是在一方表达歉意,同时另一方表示不介意时使用的,只是一种用来安抚对方的礼貌用语。正确的说法应该是"It's my pleasure."

(3)不加区别地在英语表达中使用中文的表达结构。

a. 一位美国人正在商场购物。

Chinese sales girl：What do you want?

American：(embarrassed)

销售员想用"你要点儿什么"来欢迎这位美国人。但是按照美国人的方式,在这种情况下,她应该说"Can I help you?"

b. 一位导游带领一群美国人去参观西安的一家博物馆。在他们去博物

馆的路上,他们得知不得不取消行程,因为博物馆内部装修。游客们很失望,
问导游:

Tourist：So you didn't know that beforehand, did you?

Guide：Yes.

Tourist：You didn't mean that you knew it in advance, did you?

Guide：Yes, Miss.

在这段对话中,中国导游混淆了中文和英文在回答反意疑问句时的区别。
当他回答"yes"的时候,他的意思是"Yes, I knew that beforehand.",这与他
的真实想法"I didn't know that beforehand."相反。事实上,按照英语的表达
方式,导游应该说"No, I didn't."来回答这一反意疑问句。

(4)只理解了字面意思,而没有理解说话者的真实意图。

a. 在课堂上。

Teacher：Can you work out this problem?

Student：Yes.

在英语中,"Can you..."是一个非常常见的礼貌用语表达,对母语使用者
来说,这一表达的意思是提出请求,而非询问某人做某事的能力。老师的目的
在于请这位学生来解决文中提到的问题,但是学生却将这个请求理解成了对
其能力的询问。因此,老师必然会对学生的回答感到迷惑不解。

b. 课堂上。

Teacher：Would you like to read the text?

Student：No, I wouldn't.

一般来说,母语使用者会为特定的话语赋予确切的语用用意。所以,
"Would you like to..."在英语课堂中是一个非常常见的礼貌请求或要求用
语。这样一来学生的回答就显得直接且粗鲁了。他只是将这句话看做一个普
通的问题,而没有意识到其中所包含的强烈的礼貌之意。

(5)误用完整句,忽略了造成这段话语的确切背景所暗含的意思。

a. 在托儿所。

A：Have you brought your coat?

B：Yes, I have brought my coat.

Leech 认为,完整句回答违反了语用"经济原则",而且很明显会造成不好
的印象。B 的回答会给人一种暴躁乖戾的感觉。从语用角度来看,B 违反了

合作原则的数量准则，从而会给 A 带来一种 B 的话语中并未想要表达的意思。

实际上，一些教学方法可能真的增加了这种语用失误的可能性。此类语用失误的发生可以归因为教学材料（情态的误用），课堂练习和其他一些教学导致的错误。

b. 在课堂上，老师问学生。

Teacher：Can you hear clearly?

Student：Yes，I can hear clearly.

从这段对话中也可以看出，学生误用了完整句。让人听起来感觉对方很急躁很机械。最好说成"Yes，I can."

（6）忽视了在不同的情况下要使用不同的表达。

a. A 和 B 是好朋友。A 请求 B 的帮助。A 说："Could you possibly help me with the table?" A 的语气听起来有一点陌生。好朋友之间的交流中没有必要这么拐弯抹角和保守。因此，用"Help me with the table"就可以了。

b. 在图书馆。

Professor：When shall I return this book?

Librarian：Perhaps you could read through this by Friday.

在英语中，这一表达从语用角度来讲并非总是可互换的。因此，对于地位稍低的人来说，说"Perhaps you could read through this by Friday."可以接受，也算是合适。但是，对于地位稍高于自己的人，说"Could you possibly read through this by Friday?"更加合适一些。对于母语使用者来说，"Perhaps you could"更像是要求，而非请求，而且会有一种强制或讽刺的意味。这便是目标语言的语用泛化（L2）。

综上所述，从 L1 到 L2 的言语行为策略的不当转换是造成语言语用失效的常见原因。很明显，相比纠正语法错误，外语学习者对于语言语用失效的敏感性更加微弱且不够明显。上述六种语言语用失效当然并非全部。事实上，在跨文化交际过程中，此类语用失误的来源远比我们所想的要多。在与来自不同文化的人进行交流时，我们要时刻记住，不能直接将源语言（L1）的言语行为策略转移至目标语言（L2）。要尽可能避免 L1 的干扰。

4.1.3　社交语用失误分析

社交语用失误来源于跨文化交际中对于合适的语言行为的感知存在差

异。与语言语用失误相比,社交语用失误更加难以处理,因为其中涉及说话者的信仰、渴望、意愿和他们的语言知识几乎一样多。事实上,从母语使用者和非母语使用者之间的互动中,可以很容易看出来共有的语言体系的缺失会如何导致交流的失败。地区、种族、政治和社会阶级的不同毫无疑问地反映在语用范围的多样性中,也反映在语言的变异中。

当使用的语言所处的社会环境存在差异时,便会发生社交语用失误。现已证明,不同的交际环境对说话者和听话者的社会距离、社会权利、权利及义务、特定交际行为中所涉及的强加程度要求不同。

语用期待和评估确实是具有文化特异性的。很有可能外语使用者和母语使用者所评估的强加程度、社会距离等因素是不同的。Thomas 认为:造成社交语用失误的,正是不同文化间对交际者的社会距离、交际者应该摒弃的"面子威胁行为"的尝试、交际者的权利和义务等的不同要求造成的。

在跨文化交际过程中,文化方面不合理的反应一部分与语言竞争力低有关,部分与社会文化知识水平低有关。文化方面合宜的反应方式的知识差别也可能导致社交语用失误。

跨文化评价差异导致的社交语用失误方面的例证不计其数。在这里,我们选择了几个例子,从社交语用角度分析语用失效。

(1)因忽视跨文化交流中的语境因素而导致的社交语用失误。

语境是一个动态的概念,而非静态的。语境会随环境的变化而不断变化,从广义上讲,它使得交流过程中的参与者能够互相作用,由此其互相作用中的言语表达才能够被对方理解。要想在交流中得体地使用语言,需要根据不同的场合和不同的参与者来选择不同的语言形式。

a. 王和其他同学同住一间公寓。一天,房东来收她和其他租客的房租,便和王聊了一会儿。房租交清后,房东起身准备离开。王说:"Would you like to stay a bit longer?"房东对这份"邀请"似乎有些意外,停顿了一下,说道:"No, I have something else to do. I am on my way to hospital."。

在这个例子中,王所说的"Would you like to stay a bit longer?"对于英语为母语的房东来说,是一个意料之外的邀请。由于王没有考虑到社会距离和权利关系的语境变化,这份邀请在这里显得特别奇怪。如果是在中国文化背景下,王的邀请便显得合理而且礼貌了。然而,在美国文化背景下,这么说会让对方感觉很突然,带给对方不适感。在英语环境下,当交际中涉及权利关系,比如上述房东前来向租客收取房租的情况下,对租客来说,一句"Good bye, see you later."就足够了,而且非常合适。

但是,假设情况是警察帮助居民寻找丢失的款项。当警察将找回的钱财还给失主,准备离开失主家时,失主可以说:"Would you like a cup of coffee before you go?"或是"Thank you very much. Good bye!"两种情况的区别在于,第一个案例中,房东是为了自己的利益而来的(收房租),而第二个案例中,警察来是向居民提供帮助的。

b. 英语课堂上,一位美国教授对学生说:"Before I start my lecture, I would like to give you a test in order to know where you are."听到这番话,很多学生不禁有些迷惑,问到:"Why, Professor, we are in the classroom."

如果我们把这段对话放在特定的语境下进行分析,就能明显看出学生犯了社交语用失误的错误。他们只理解了这句话的字面意思,或者说这句话在普遍语境下的自然意义(教授想知道他们在哪里)。但是他们没有理解其中暗含的意思,或者说话者的意思(教授想知道的是学生目前的英文水平)。如果在交际中有一方没有理解语境暗示,他/她就无法对针对问题做出相关的回答。

语言交际是一种复杂的活动,只有当来自不同文化背景的参与者对所处的语境存在共识时,才能达到交际的目的,否则就会发生误解。

(2)文化价值观不同导致的社交语用失误。

如果说语言语用失误属于表层,那么社交语用失误就属于深层。大部分社交语用失误是由于文化价值观的概念差异而导致的。

大部分难以解决的语用失误都是由于语用原则,比如礼貌原则与其他有着深刻影响的价值,比如真诚原则或真实原则发生冲突而引起的。

Leech 认为:不能否认的是,语用原则会将交际价值观——比如真实原则——引入语言的研究中。传统上,语言学家会尽量避免涉及这些价值观,觉得会颠覆一直声称的客观性。但是,从实证的角度来看,只要在研究中所涉及的价值观是在社交活动中确实存在的,而非我们强加于社交活动的,那就没有必要在考量的时候排除这些因素。

文化价值观是我们行为的基础。文化价值观能够指导我们的行为,帮助我们分辨是非善恶。价值体系因文化不同而存在差异,并且决定了不同文化之间的交际行为差异。

a. 一位中国警察向他的英国上司请假,要带他的母亲去医院。对话如下:

Chinese policeman：Sir?

British superior：Yes，what is it?

Chinese policeman：My mother is not very well，Sir.

British superior：So?

Chinese policeman：She has to go into hospital，Sir.

British superior：Well，get on with it. What do you want?

Chinese policeman：On Thursday，Sir.

British superior：Bloody hell，man. What do you want?

Chinese policeman：Nothing，Sir.

大多数中国人会觉得英国警官没有人情味。而本土英国人则会觉得中国警察很讨厌，不够坦诚。这个案例中语用失误的原因很明显。中国警察想请假带他母亲去医院。按照中国文化，作为上司，英国警官应表达对中国警察的关心，并准假。然而，在英国文化中，某人母亲是否生病事实上与其他人无关。英国警官想知道的是中国警察到底需要什么。总而言之，文化价值观不同导致了上述语用失误。

一些言语行为对于来自其他文化的人来说会显得粗鲁、不礼貌，但对于本文化的人来说缺失理所当然、合情合理的，是本文化中约定俗成的惯例。跨文化交际中的实际困难在于文化误解。例如，在英语文化中，用单一的行为（直接回答"是"或"不是"）进行应答并完成一项邀请或提议是非常自然且礼貌的，但是在中国文化中，要想有礼貌就需要一系列的行为。对于中国人来说，一项邀请或提议发出后会得到拒绝的反馈，然后一方再进行邀请，如此进行几个回合也是非常常见的。

在某些文化中被认为是道德上良好或社会层面有用的情感或行为在另外一些文化中可能会是不好或无用的，那么用来描述特定行为的词汇或言语表达便会具有不同的情感意义。在中国文化中，针对特定的个人问题做出的直接评论或问题会显得友好且合适，但在英语文化中则是不可接受甚至具有侵犯性的。举个例子，中国人可能会对朋友说："哦，你这条裙子比我那天买的贵多了，不划算的。"这类话语对于中国人来说会显得很友好，但对于英语文化中的人来说，会让听话者觉得低于他人，因而具有侵犯性。

再举一个例子，中国人会对许久不见的朋友说："你还是老样子，一点也没变。"假设这位中国人对美国朋友说："Hello，haven't seen you for ages! You haven't changed at all!"这么说一定会让母语为英语的人感到被冒犯了，因为暗示了他/她缺乏变化，或者没有进步。美国文化中的真理在于"变化"。在美国人眼里，"变化"包含了打破传统、敢于创新的精神。"变化"意味着"发展"和"进步"。而中国人倡导"稳定"，并在"稳定"中寻求进步和发展。这种文化价值观念与美国文化中的冒险和进取精神大相径庭。

在某些文化中人们乐于讨论的话题，在另一些文化中则是人们会极力避免的：也是在另一些文化中人们认为会侵犯到他人隐私的话题。在中国文化中，收入、宗教信仰、婚姻状态都是可以谈论的话题，并无什么限制。但是在英语文化中，这些话题很明显会威胁到个人隐私。总而言之，社交语用失效来源于文化差异。下面这些例子更能够说明这一论点。

b. A：Here is some little thing for you，but it's not very good.

B：No，no. I really can't accept.

A：But you must. It was bought specially for you.

B：No，no，no，I can't … I won't take it.

A：Oh，come on，take it.

B：(taking it slowly) oh，all right，you really shouldn't have gone to the expense.

在这个例子中，A 是一个美国人。他给他的中国朋友买了个礼物。他不满意 B 的反应，因为 B 没有意识到接受礼物时的不同态度。在英语文化中，当一个人得到一份礼物时，他倾向于打开包装并看一看，这表示接受者对送礼者的尊重。在中国文化中，打开礼品盒是不礼貌的。礼物也许不值钱，所以当场打开礼物可能会让对方丢脸。

在日常的跨文化中交流中，可见大量的跨文化价值冲突的例子。除了前面提到的例子，我们经常看见美国人使用这样的例子，比如："We really must get together sometime."对于美国人来说，他们仅仅是出于礼貌，这些话并没有意义，但是非美国人常把它当作是真正的邀请，在得知事实并不是这样的时候感到很伤心。这只是随口说说而已。因此，非美国人认为这是美国人伪善的一面，伪善也被认为是非美国人愤怒和沮丧的源头。如果这样的表达提及到时间、地点或活动，那么它可能被视为一个"真正的"邀请。

总之，语用语言失误和社会语言失误在跨文化交际过程中并存，前者是交际失误的表层结构，而后者是交际失误的深层结构。首先是语言的特定性，教师负责纠正它们。其次是文化特殊性，这反映了学生的价值观和信仰体系。除了用一些方法来培养学生的文化意识外，很难加以纠正。作为英语老师和学生，他们必须找出原因并找到方法来避免它们。

4.2　语用失误成因

经过实例分析,笔者认为语用失误产生的原因主要有以下几个方面:

第一,二语学习者并不总是把通用的语用知识或第一语言基础上的语用知识的某些方面转移到第二语言交际中去。他们倾向于理解话语的表面价值,而不是推断其潜在含义。他们通常不利用上下文信息。在第一语言情境下,有证据表明,二语学习者在选择语用策略时往往对语境非常敏感。然而,他们不能很好地区分第二语言情境中社会距离和权力的语境变量。

比如,当一个英国人要离开的时候,他可能会说"I am sorry, I can't stay long." "Thank you for a wonderful evening." 或者"It was nice seeing you." 为了回应这一点,许多中国人只翻译汉语问候客套话的字面意思,而不考虑上下文因素。如:"Would you like to stay a bit longer?"(不多坐一会儿吗?)在两个朋友的聚会上,当一个人注意到另一个人情绪低落,即将离开时,这个人会说"Never mind, you could stay a bit longer."如果他们的社会距离很近,没有涉及权力关系,主人会说:"Come again when you have time." 但当涉及权力关系时,如果准备要离开的时候,主人说"Would you like to stay a bit longer?",客人可能会想"for what?"

第二,第一语言语用知识的负迁移可能也会造成失误。这表现在两个方面。不适当的迁移会发生在语言语用层面。当说话者试图从第一语言转移到第二语言时,这种情况就会发生。这在语义或句法上是等价的,但是由于不同的解释倾向,它将在目标语中产生不同的语用作用。

另一方面,负迁移也会发生在社会语用层面。有人认为社交语用失误是跨文化交际中社会距离、权力关系、社会价值观的错配造成的。这些错配反过来影响着语言选择。非本族语者可能会以与本族语者不同的方式判断相对权力或社会距离。这些差异在两种不同文化的师生交流中表现得最为明显。在学生自己的文化中,教师在英语文化背景中的地位要高于他们。这个社会判断导致学生通常表现得比预期恭敬。例如,在西方国家,教师和学生是同龄人。他们的关系中没有涉及太多的社会距离和相对权力。这就是美国学生敢于挑战教师权威的原因。他们可能会提一些直接的问题或表达来反驳老师。在中国文化中,教师受到高度尊重。一句中国谚语"一日为师终身为父"很好地体现了这个宗旨。许多中国学生害怕挑战老师的权威,即使他们对老师的想法有疑惑。例如,在一节英语课结束后,一个中国学生对美国老师说:"Mr.

Grey，you've made a wonderful lecture!"中国学生违背了品质准则，让别人觉得他在刻意奉承，显得有点虚伪。

第三，语用失误可能与教学因素有关。有人认为，尤其是在英语情境下使用的教材和课话语缺乏真实性。目前，对元语言知识的过分强调表明某一语法范畴与言语行为之间存在一一对应关系。在例子"So much for page 10"中，语用失误主要是由课堂教学中不真实的输入引起的。它也可能是学习者只被教授了语言形态，而没有意识到它们的语用作用。教师在英语语法教学中很少增加语用知识。以"to be ＋ inf."结构的教学为例。教师不仅要告诉学生这种结构的一些用法，还应该告诉学生这个结构通常与第二人称主体连用，表明说话人与听话人是上下级关系。其目的是在这个句子"You're to be here by eight."中发出一个命令。

4.3　语用能力测试

4.3.1　测试目的

自从 1972 年美国社会语言学家 Dell Hymes 出版了《论交际能力》一书，人们就开始关注语言在各种语境中的应用。许多外语教师也意识到培养交际能力的重要性。在跨文化交际的过程中，研究交际中的障碍对外语教学也越来越重要。在过去的 20 年里，外语教学研究领域的一些专家在英汉语用差异方面取得了一些成果，如胡文仲、邓炎昌和刘润清、何自然和闫庄、王得杏、洪刚。但很少有人来研究与非英语专业学生的语法能力和语用能力相关的语用失误。

由于跨文化交际过程中语用失误的增多，我们对外语学习者在跨文化交际中的语用失误进行了测试。我们借助一些语用学理论对受试者的成绩进行了分析和说明。测试的目的在于：①受试者在哪些领域和方面会犯语用错误。②语言能力较强的学生是否具有较强的语用能力。换句话说，学生的语言能力与语用能力是否成正比。③研究语用失误对英语学习和教学的启示，探讨中国学生在跨文化交际过程中避免语用失误的有效策略。

4.3.2　理论依据

本研究旨在探讨学生语言能力与语用能力的关系，能力包括语法能力和交际能力。语法能力通过 Chomsky 的作品得到了普及，然后被解释为语言教学和学习的唯一目的。研究发现,语言受到诸多社会文化因素的制约,学习语言不仅仅是熟记规则和单词。交际能力的概念已经演变为语法能力的补充。语法能力是指语言系统,而交际能力是指语言的使用。从广义上讲,跨文化交际过程中强调交际能力,它的语用功能和语用能力一样重要。在这个意义上,我们可以把交际能力和语用能力等同起来。

进行调查时,我们采用了 Jenny Thomas 的观点,即语用失误可分为两大类:语用语言失误和社会语言失误。所有的问题都是根据这些理论依据进行选择和整理的。

4.3.3 方法

本研究的研究对象为西安理工大学理工科两个班的大二学生和研究生。有 26 名研究生,30 名来自英语水平较高的 A 班学生和 29 名来自英语水平相对较低的 B 班学生。A 班学生来自管理系,B 班学生来自水利水电系,在他们被选为研究对象前,对他们进行了能力测试(见表 4.1)。

表 4.1 英语能力测试统计

研究对象	各项分数				
	听力	阅读	词汇	完形填空	平均数
研究生	15.6	34.2	15.2	16.2	81.2
A 班	14.4	30.5	13.4	14	72.3
B 班	13.7	28.7	11.3	14.8	68.5

研究生平均得分为 81.2 分,A 班的平均分为 72.3 分,B 的平均分为 68.5 分(总分为 100 分)。从表 4.1 我们可以看出,研究生的语法能力排名第一,而 B 班学生的语法能力排在最后,A 班学生的语法能力处于中等水平。本研究选取这三组学生作为研究样本,试图了解语言能力较好的学生在测试中是否具有较好的语用能力,语言表达能力较强的学生在跨文化交际过程中的语用失误是否较少。

语用能力测试包含 20 个多项选择题,分为两组。第一组主要是语用语言的问题,从第一题到第十题。第二组是社交语用问题,从第十一题到第二十题。语用语言的问题主要是用于测试两方面的能力。一方面是理解某些话语语用含义的能力。另一方面是在特定语境下表达自己意图或理解他人意图的能力。社会语用问题主要是用来测试学生根据交互对象的不同文化背景和社会环境,使用适当的语言表达能力。

测试问题的收集和编辑来自于以下渠道:①上海外语教育出版社出版的《大学英语听力教程》中的一些问题;②作者多年来的个人教学经验;③与作者一个部门的老师也提出了一些问题;④几个问题选自何自然和闫庄的研究。

这个测试是分三天进行的。学生要在 30 分钟内完成测试。如果遇到陌生且难懂的词,他们可以查字典,这样可以避免因语法和语义理解困难而造成的语用失误。

4.3.4　结果与分析(见表 4.2 和表 4.3)

表 4.2　语用能力测试分数分布

研究对象	得分占比情况				
	<50	50～59	60～69	70～79	80～89
研究生	5/26	7/26	10/26	3/26	1/26
A 班	1/30	7/30	8/30	9/30	5/30
B 班	6/29	8/29	12/29	3/29	0/29

表 4.3　三个层次研究对象的分数

研究对象	研究生	A 班	B 班
最高分	80	95	80
最低分	50	60	55
平均分	62.3	75.3	62.1

结果如上述两表所示。从表 4.2 我们可以看出,26 名研究生中有 12 名分数在 59 分以下,A 班 30 名学生中 8 名分数在 59 分以下,B 班 29 名学生中 14 名分数在 59 分以下。换句话说,错误率分别为 46％,27％和 48％。此外,60 分以上的,研究生有 14 人,A 班有 22 人,B 班有 15 人。这表明,及格率分别为 54％,73％和 52％。在 70～89 分的范围内,研究生有 4 人,A 班有 14 人,B

班有 3 人,他们的比例分别是 15％、47％和 10％。

从表 4.2 可以得出一些结论。第一,我们发现 A 班的学生成绩最好。第二,与 B 类学生相比,研究生没有取得更好的成绩。换言之,两组在语用成绩上差异不显著。第三,这表明三组受试者的语用能力与他们各自的语言能力不一致。

表 4.2 还表明 A 班的学生在测试中表现最好,而研究生则表现相对较差,尽管他们的语法能力被认为是三组学生中最好的。根据调查,有超过 50％的研究生是在大学毕业后的 2～5 年内继续深造。他们没有太多的精力、时间和机会去学习跨文化语用知识。A 班和 B 班的学生在学校待的时间较长,他们学到了更多的文化知识与语用原则。有一个例外是 B 班的学生主要来自边远山区。他们在语法能力和语用能力上都不突出。但我们可以看出研究生的语用能力与他们的语用能力的差异并不显著。

表 4.3 表明 A 类的学生获得了最高分,而一名研究生获得了最低分,这令人有点吃惊。平均分数表明研究生成绩几乎和 B 班的学生一样差。

表 4.4 是三组学生完成的 20 个问题的错误率。第一,从这张表可以看出三组学生的成绩一点也不令人满意。第二,85 名受试者中,没有一个达到满分。三组学生关于这 20 个问题错误率的差异并不显著。第三,三组学生在在语用失误的某些方面几乎都有共同点。第四,这些问题的平均错误率是不同的,A 班学生的错误率最低,研究生最高。同时,研究生的错误率几乎和 B 班学生一样,这令人有点吃惊。

表 4.4　三组学生中 20 个问题的错误率

题号	学生的错误率		
	研究生	A 班	B 班
1	46％	43％	41％
2	55％	42％	51％
3	33％	39％	43％
4	34％	32％	41％
5	55％	47％	46％
6	43％	51％	53％
7	45％	42％	52％

续 表

题号	学生的错误率		
	研究生	A 班	B 班
8	63%	62%	67%
9	51%	49%	51%
10	45%	38%	40%
11	54%	57%	61%
12	39%	35%	32%
13	45%	35%	37%
14	38%	29%	35%
15	29%	32%	27%
16	40%	35%	36%
17	50%	41%	43%
18	34%	28%	33%
19	41%	28%	34%
20	57%	55%	52%
平均数	45%	41%	44%

问题 1～10 是关于语言本身的语用问题。在第 5 个问题中，一位美国女士踩到一名中国年轻人说："I am terribly sorry."要求学生们对她的道歉做出适当的回答。在 85 名学生中，有 64 名学生（75%）选择"It doesn't matter."只有 5 名学生（6%）选择"That's all right."作为回答。在第 8 个问题中，一位美国人对中国同伴说，"That's very kind of you.",有 62 名学生选择"Never mind."作为回答。英语"Never mind."和汉语"没关系"的字面含义相似，但是它们用在不同的场合有不同的语用功能。在中国，"没关系"可以用作对对方"赞赏"和"道歉"的回答。例如，"太感谢你了！"—"没关系"或"实在对不起"—"没关系。"在英语中，"Never mind."只能用来回答"道歉"。调查结果表明，学生最常犯的错误在于使用某些固定词组。特别是汉语和英语中

的一些固定词组同时具有相似的字面意思。

问题 11～20 是关于社交语用失误的。一般来说,社交语用失误主要是由中国文化和英语文化之间的差异引起的。以测试中的问题 11 为例。一位美国顾客想买一些龙井茶,但茶叶已经卖完了。对话如下:

Customer：Do you have Longjing tea?

Salesgirl：Oh, no, we run out.

Customer：Oaky, thanks anyway.

Salesgirl：...

至于答案,多达 75％的学生选择"You are welcome",这相当于汉语的"不用谢"。在中国,客户习惯于表现出对服务的感谢。与此相反,在西方国家,店员应该感谢顾客的来访,当他们不能给客户提供一些服务时,他们应该表达他们的道歉。所以女店员应该说"I am sorry"。

从表 4.4 可见关于问题 20 的错误率是非常高的。研究生、A 班学生和 B 班学生的错误率分别为 57％、55％和 52％。语境是:在去服装表演的路上,一位英国经理的妻子正在和一位秘书谈话。当妻子说"It's really cold tonight"时,大多数学生认为秘书应该说:"Here, take my jacket",这是不正确的。原因是学生不知道"It's really cold tonight"实际上是美国文化中朋友之间的问候,而不是需要衣服。所以在这里学生违反了礼貌原则。

根据测试结果可知在不同的文化背景下的礼貌原则造成的语用语言失误和社会语用失误是不难克服的。我们可以把它们看作是表面结构上的语用失误。另一方面,源自深层文化心理层面的社交语用失误是很难克服的。例如,外国人对中国人的赞美。因为"谦虚"这个概念已经深深扎根于中国人的头脑中,即使他们知道如何回应外国人的称赞,他们也习惯于拒绝。这是由于英国人和中国人在深层文化心理上的差异。

总之,结合四个表,我们可以看到研究生可能对语法、词汇或语言能力掌握得比较好,但他们的文化知识可能不太丰富和健全,从而导致他们的语用能力较差。研究生与 B 类学生在语用能力方面的成绩没有显著差异,尽管这两组学生的语言能力处于不同水平。这表明,高水平的语法能力并不能保证高水平的语用能力。

调查结果表明:语言知识的大量输入并不一定会引起语言应用和语用能力的相应提高。受试者由于缺乏语用能力,从而导致了语用语言失误和社交语言失误。

4.4 语用能力和语用失误相关的问卷调查

设计这部分问卷是要研究对象反馈他们对培养语用能力的重要性如何看待,以及看看他们在跨文化交际过程中如何回答语用失误问题。选择的研究对象来自西安理工大学 A 班和 B 班各 15 名学生。

问卷调查有 8 个问题。前 7 道题都是是-非问题,主要有关语用失误的一些方面以及学生对语用能力的看法,最后一题是一道简答题。研究对象的回答和第二部分中假设的答案总体一致(见表 4.5)。

表 4.5 问卷调查结果

问题	班级回答占比情况	
	A 班	B 班
1	53%——否	73%——否
2	67%——语用失误	73%——语用失误
3	60%——否	67%——否
4	80%——语言能力	60%——语言能力
5	60%——否	67%——否
6	87%——测试	87%——测试
7	80%——否	87%——否

从表 4.5 中,我们可以看出一些东西很有意思。具体来讲,第一道题,A 班有 8 名(53%)学生、B 班有 11 名(73%)学生选择了"否"。当问学生在和美国人交流时,什么使得他们倍感紧张,A 班 10 名(67%)学生、B 班 11 名(73%)学生选择了语用失误。这表明,学生已经觉得,在交际中语用失误要比语法失误更为严重。另外,第三个问题中,A 班有 9 名(60%)学生、B 班有 10 名(67%)学生选择了"否"。这表明,学生不满意当前的教学方法。对第四题,A 班有 12 名(80%)学生、B 班有 9 名(60%)学生认为,在英语学习中语言能力比语用能力更为重要。之后,我和他们进行了讨论。许多学生说精通语言技能会让他们在大学英语四级和六级考试中得分更高。第五题,A 班有 9 名

（60％）学生、B 班有 10 名（67％）学生考虑说，他们很少读一些英语读物来扩展自身文化知识。第六题的回答中，A 班和 B 班各有 13 名（87％）学生均认为，目前的大学生英语四级和六级考试体系使得他们忽略了对语用能力的培养。这表明，当前的语言考试系统应该改革，把学生引导向正确的语言学习道路。问题七，A 班 12 名（80％）学生、B 班 13 名（87％）学生选择了"否"。这意味着教师上课时很少向学生们教授语用知识。究其原因，部分在于当前非母语英语课程的教学体系，部分在于教师本身就教学能力不足。

就最后一道题，所有学生都回答说，老师应该注重培养学生的语用能力，同时也不忽视对学生语法能力的训练。他们期望老师能教一些语用策略来避免语用错误。同时也希望，能提供给他们更多与外国人交流的机会。他们认为，在语言教学的过程中也应该传授文化知识。

从这次调查可以总结出，学生对于语用失误和语用能力的态度还是积极的。遗憾的是，因为目前应试型的语言考试体系和教学方法，学生不得不花大量时间加强自身语言能力，容易忽视对自己语用能力的培养。这就是近几年语用失误在非母语英语学习者之中如此普遍的主要原因。

CHAPTER 5   CULTIVATION OF INTER-CULTURAL PRAGMATIC COMPETENCE

In the process of cultivation of learners' pragmatic competence, some strategies and approaches need to be adopted to reduce and avoid pragmatic failures. To reduce and avoid pragmatic failures is closely connected with English learning and teaching methodology. Therefore, some approaches and suggestions are put forward for the enhancement and cultivation of learners' pragmatic competence.

As people speak, they always take some strategies so as to achieve the general objective of communication. Therefore, language communication can be summarized as the application of strategy. Without effective communicative strategy, pragmatic failures cannot be avoided essentially. Tarone defines communicative strategy as mutual attempts of two interlocutors to agree on a meaning in situations where requisite meaning structures do not seem to be shaked. A communication strategy is a shared enterprise in which both the speaker and the hearer are involved rather than being only the responsibility of the speaker. When the two participants realize that they are not understanding each other, they will resort to some ways to help them out.

The author maintains that pragmatic strategies equal communicative strategies to some extent. The mastery of communication strategies is an indispensable portion of pragmatic competence.

5.1   Reasons to Develop Pragmatic Competence

The overview and analysis of pragmatic failures can not only contribute to a clear and comprehensive understanding of pragmatic failures, they also suggest that L2 learners' pragmatic ability needs pedagogical training. The conscious development of pragmatic ability is based on the following grounds.

First of all, learners' pragmatic ability is part of their communicative competence. According to Bachman, language competence is composed of two elements, "organizational competence" and "pragmatic competence". Organizational competence refers to the knowledge of linguistic units and the rules of joining them together at the levels of sentence (grammatical competence) and discourse (textual competence). Pragmatic competence is made up of illocutionary competence and sociolinguistic competence. The former includes knowledge of communicative action and the ability about how to carry it out; the latter comprises the ability to use language appropriately according to the context.

As indicated in Bachman's model, pragmatic competence is not an extra or a luxury, but a necessary component of communicative competence and interacts with organizational competence in complex ways. Hence it follows that in order to communicate effectively in L2, the learners' pragmatic competence must be reasonably developed.

Secondly, making a pragmatic error is far more serious than a linguistic one. Bardovi-Harlig and Hardford find that non-native speakers usually tend to be more definite and assertive when compared to the tentativeness that characterizes the native speakers' suggestions. "I will take", and "I want to make" are in strong contrast with the native use of "I was thinking" and "I would like to". They point out that the non-native speakers' inappropriate expressions make them appear "pushy" or "rude". Thomas summarizes the effect caused by inadequately developed pragmatic competence: "Grammatical errors may reveal a speaker to be a less than proficient language user; pragmatic failures reflect badly on him or her as a person." More often than not, a native speaker could attribute L2 learner's impoliteness to boorishness or ill-will rather than any linguistic deficiency.

Thirdly, foreign language teaching fails to prepare learners' pragmatic competence. According to my previous research, there is an imbalance between learners' grammatical and pragmatic competence, with the latter falling behind the former. It is especially true for advanced L2 learners (see Table 4.1 and Table 4.2 of the survey). From the survey we can see quite a number of students' utterances are linguistically correct, but pragmatically inappropriate. Without a pragmatic focus, foreign language teaching may help to develop learners' grammatical competence, but may not contribute to developing learners' pragmatic competence.

5.2 Pedagogical Principles and Approaches to the Development of Pragmatic Competence

The achievement of language, however, is not simply in the mastery of the forms of language, but the mastery of forms in order to accomplish the communicative functions of language. Mastery of vocabulary and structures results in nothing if the learner cannot use those forms for the purpose of transmitting and receiving thoughts, ideas, and feelings between speaker and hearer, or writer and reader. While forms are the manifestation of language, functions are the realization of those forms. The pragmatic purpose of language — the use of signs and symbols for communication — is thus the final and ultimate objective of the EFL learner.

As far as pedagogical principles are concerned, a focus on communicative language teaching — teaching foreign languages for the ultimate goal of communication with native speakers of the foreign language is made. Such a focus has centered on speaking and listening skills, on writing for specific communicative purposes, and on "authentic" reading texts. Underlying the communicative language teaching movement are a number of important theoretical principles of language behavior. Unfortunately even in the present EFL teaching context, the traditional teaching approach, or the grammar-translation method is still adopted and practiced. Its' principal characteristics is that language is taught first through detailed analysis of its grammar, followed by translating the sentences or the text into or out of the target language. The students use the first language as the medium system in the acquisition of a foreign language. Vocabulary selection is based solely on the reading texts used, and words are taught through bilingual word list, dictionary study. Grammar-translation method is a teacher-centered method and ignores the function of communication to a large degree. In contrast to the traditional teaching method, communicative language teaching pays systematic attention to functional as well as structural aspects of language. The four interconnected characteristics are: ① Classroom goals are focused on all of the components of communicative competence and not restricted to grammatical or linguistic competence. ② Form is not the primary framework for organizing and sequencing lessons. Function is the framework through which forms are taught. ③ Accuracy is secondary to conveying a message. Fluency may take on more importance than accuracy. The ultimate criterion for communicative success is the actual transmission and receiving of intended meaning. ④ In the communicative classroom, students ultimately have to use the language productively and receptively in an unrehearsed contexts.

The awkward situation on the part of EFL learners calls for the pedagogical intervention. Indeed there are some problems in the teaching of culture and pragmatics. First, the study of pragmatic knowledge involves time that many teachers do not feel they can spare in an already overcrowded curriculum. Teachers often satisfy themselves with the thought that students will be exposed to cultural materials later, after they have mastered the basic grammar and vocabulary of the language. Unfortunately, "later" never seems to come for most students. Secondly, many teachers are afraid to teach pragmatic knowledge and strategy because they fear that they don't know enough about them. Lastly, many teachers hold that the teaching of pragmatics and culture involves dealing with students' attitudes. Many students assume that for every word in the native language there is an exact equivalent in the target language. Some think that the foreign language is t he same as the native language, except that it uses different words.

Given such situations in EFL teaching and learning, some effective approaches and enlightening suggestions that can help develop pragmatic competence are recommended.

(1) A kind of tendency should be avoided in the course of EFL teaching, that is, linguistic knowledge is usually taught prior to the teaching of language application. This tendency will result in the outcome that EFL learners apply mechanically the rules of speech function in the mother language to the different contexts in the course of intercultural communication, which leads to the failure of communication. The teachers should keep balance between the traditional teaching method and modern

teaching method, with the former stressing the teaching of grammatical knowledge and the latter the cross-cultural and pragmatic knowledge.

(2) The teaching materials should be made more authentic. It has better to say that authenticity does not lie in the text but in the uses speakers and users make of it. According to Widdowson, it is probably better to consider authenticity not as a quality residing in instances of language but as a quality which is bestowed upon them, created by the response of the receiver. Authenticity in this view is a function of the interaction between the reader/ hearer and the text which incorporates the intentions of the writer/speaker. Authenticity has to do with appropriate response. Perhaps one of the main authentic activities within a language classroom is communication about how best to learn to communicate. Perhaps the most authentic language learning tasks are those which require the learner to undertake communication and metacommunication. Native speakers' input is essential for pragmatic learning. It is not that the native speaker should be a model of EFL learners' speech behavior, but rather it helps them to build their own pragmatic knowledge on the right kind of input. In addition, as language is laden with socio-cultural values, it would be very helpful for developing EFL learners' cross-cultural pragmatic competence in particular if they can get regular exposure to authentic materials.

(3) The classroom can become more student-centered and interactive in nature. Small group work requires students to take alternating discourse roles as speakers and listeners, and different tasks engage students in different speech events and communicative actions. For example, activities like role-play, simulation and drama may get students involved in different social roles and speech events. These situational practices are excellent for providing natural, authentic linguistic exchanges that include paralinguistic information as well. They can be used to demonstrate not only conventional language in a variety of survival situations, but also certain conventional gestures and other cultural features, such as appropriate social distance, eye contact, and the like.

(4) A pragmatic consciousness-raising approach can be used to develop pragmatic competence in EFL contexts. This approach sensitizes learners to context-based variations in language use and the factors that contribute to those variations, rather than teach a specific means of performing a speech

act. In EFL contexts, classroom settings and the use of video can help to raise EFL learners' pragmatic consciousness. Outside the classroom, English teachers may hold lectures introducing English cultures, conventions, and history. Students should be given more chances to communicate with the native English teachers. By interacting with the foreign teachers, students can learn something they can't learn in the classroom.

(5) EFL teachers should strive to be bicultural, or at least familiar with the target culture. It is far from enough to explain the literal meaning and language forms. Most important of all, the teachers should give a detailed explanation for the different pragmatic functions of language forms and their uses in different contexts. The teachers should consciously reflect cultural perspectives in the course of teaching. For instance, using cultural information when teaching vocabulary, teaching students about the connotative meaning of new words, grouping vocabulary into culture-related clusters. In teaching the culture of target language, teachers should not only instill the knowledge into the students. More importantly, they should organize the students into groups to make the comparison and contrast between the Chinese and the English culture. The students' cultural sensitivity and pragmatic competence could be improved in this way.

(6) It is necessary to reform the present language testing system. Not only the students' linguistic ability should be tested, but their corresponding communicative and pragmatic ability should also be tested. A communicative test has to meet some rather stringent criteria. It has to test for grammatical, discourse, sociolinguistic, and illocutionary competence as well as strategic competence. It has to be pragmatic in that it requires the learner to use language naturally for genuine communication and to relate to thoughts and feelings, in short, to put authentic language to use within a context. It should test the learner in a variety of language functions. This kind of test may guide the students positively to attach importance to the difference between the Chinese culture and the English culture, the cultural connotation of lexical terms in the two languages, and to learn how to express themselves properly on different occasions.

第 5 章　跨文化语用能力的培养

在培养语言学习者的语用能力中,必须采用一些方法和策略来减少和避免语用失误。减少和避免语用失误在很大程度上与英语外语学习和教学相关联。为此,作者对英语外语学习者语用能力的培养和提升提出了一些建议和方法。

正如人们所言,为了达到交流的大体目的,经常会采取一些策略。因此,语言交流可概括为交际策略的应用。没有有效的交际策略,就无法从根本上避免语用失误。Tarone 将交际策略定义为:对话者两人表面上不破坏社交场合中的必要意义结构,在其中就某一意义达成共识的共同尝试。这条交际策略就像股份制企业,说话者与听话者都参与进去,而非说话者一人之责。当交际者二人意识到互相不能理解时,就会借助一些方法使其摆脱困境。

我们认为,语用策略在一定程度上就相当于交际策略。掌握交际策略是语用能力中不可少的一部分。

5.1　发展语用能力的原因

对语用失误的概述和分析不仅可助于清楚、全面了解语用失误,也表明外语学习者的语用能力需要教学法方面的培训。有意识地培养语用能力有以下几点原因。

第一,学习者的语用能力是他们交际能力的一部分。根据 Bachman 的观点,语言能力由两个要素组成:组织能力和语用能力。组织能力是指语言单位知识以及将语言单位组合成句子(语法能力)及语篇(语篇能力)的法则。语用能力由言外语言能力和社会语言能力构成。前者包括交际行为的知识和如何执行交际行为的能力;后者包括根据上下文恰当使用语言的能力。

如 Bachman 的模型所述,语用能力并非额外的能力,也非高级能力,而是交际能力必须的组成部分,并且和组织能力错综复杂地互相作用着。由此可得出结论,为了有效地用外语进行交流,必须好好培养学习者的语用能力。

第二,犯一个语用错误要比犯一个语言错误严重得多。Bardovi Harlig 和 Hardford 发现,比起说母语者的意见中特有的犹疑语气,非母语者说话往往会更加笃定和独断。他们往往使用"I will take"和"I want to make",这比起母语使用者"I was thinking"和"I would like to"就形成了强烈反差。他们指出,非母语者不恰当的表达使得自己看上去既"莽撞"又"粗鲁"。Thomas 总结了语用能力培养不当造成的后果:"语法失误可能会暴露说话人不是一个语言运用高手,但语用失误会反映出他(或她)为人差劲。"通常,说母语的人可能会将外语学习者的失礼看作是鲁莽或恶意为之,而不是任何语言上的不足。

第三,外语教学未能给学习者进行语用能力教育训练。根据之前的研究,学习者的语法能力和语用错误之间存在着不平衡,后者落后于前者。这对程度较高的外语学习者来说确实如此(见调查表 4.1 和表 4.2)。从调查可知,相当多的学生的说话方式在语言上是正确的,但语用上不准确。不注重语用,外语教学就只能促进对学习者语法能力的培养,而不会对其培养语用能力有所助益。

5.2　培养语用能力的教学原则和方法

然而,语言所取得的成就不仅仅是掌握语言的形式,而是掌握了其形式以实现语言的交际功能。如果学习者不会使用这些形式去传递或接收说话人与听话人、抑或作者与读者之间的思想、意见或情感,那掌握词汇和句子结构也没有任何意义。形式表现了语言,同时功能也使这些形式得以体现。语言的语用目的——使用符号和代号来交流,也就是英语学习者的终极目标了 。

就教学原则而言,已经确定了交际语言教学的重点——为了和外语母语说话人交流的终极目标而教外语。该重点的中心是以说、听为技巧,以交际目的而写作,以达正宗而读文。和交际语言教学相关的,就是许多重要的语言行为的理论原则了。遗憾的是,就算在当前的 EFL 英语教学情境之中,还依然采用和践行着传统教学方法或语法翻译法。它的主要特点是,教语言先要详细分析语法,再把句子或文本翻译成目标语。学生在外语学习过程中把母语作为中介系统。选择词汇仅仅是根据用到的阅读文本,(老师)教单词通过双语单词表和字典学习。语法翻译法以教师为中心,很大程度上忽略了交际的功能。相比于传统教学方法,交际语言教学重视语言的功能和结构方面。其四个互相联系的特点是:①课堂教学目的以交际能力的所有要素为重,不局限于语法能力或语言能力。②（语言）形式不是课堂组织和课堂秩序的基础架构，（语言）功能才是，通过功能教形式。③信息（流利）传达第一，精确第二。流畅要比精确更为重要。④交际课堂中，学生在新情景中最终还得创造性和接受性地使用语言。

克服英语学习者的窘境需要新的教学法参与进来。文化教学和语用教学中确实存在很多问题。首先，语用知识学习需要时间，老师们觉得在已经课满为患的情况下挤不出多余的时间来。老师们确信，待学生们掌握了基本的语言的语法和词汇之后，他们就会接触到文化资源。遗憾的是，对大多数学生来说就再也没有"之后"了。其次，很多老师不敢教语用知识和策略，因为担心自己所知道的语用知识和策略也不多。最后，很多老师认为，语用学教学和文化教学牵扯到要克服学生的态度。很多学生想当然地认为，母语中的每个单词在目标语中都有一个确切的对等词。一些学生认为，外语和母语除了使用的词语不一样外其余都是一样的。

在非母语英语的教和学中设定这样的情境，介绍了一些有效的方法和启发性的建议，能帮助培养语用能力。

（1）在非母语英语教学中应该避免一种倾向：教语言应用之前通常要先教语言学知识。这种倾向会导致一种后果，英语学习者在跨文化交际中，会把母语中的言语功能法则机械地应用到不同的情境之中去，导致交流失败。老师应该保持传统教学方法和现代教学方法之间相平衡，而前者重在教语法知识，后者强调教跨文化知识和语用知识。

（2）教学材料应该更加真实可靠。与其说真实性源于文本，不如说源于说话者在语言使用过程中的具体用途。据 Widdowson 所言，不应把真实性看作是存在于语言的实体之中的属性，而应看作它被赋予一种特征可能会更好一点，而这种特征实际上是语言使用者的自然反应。这样看来，真实性就是读者（听者和包含着作者）说话者意图的文本之间互动的一种功能，语言的真实性与语言使用者的真实反应紧密联系。也许语言课堂中主要的真实活动之一就是讨论学习交流的最好办法。最真实的语言学习任务也许就是要求学习者进行信息交流和元信息传递。说母语的人进行信息投入是语用学习的关键。母语说话者不应是非母语英语学习者的言语行为模范，而应是用正确的信息输入帮助学习者们建立他们自己的语用知识（体系）。另外，语言充满了社会文化价值，如果英语学习者可以经常接触正宗的（语言）资料，该语言会非常有助于培养英语学习者的跨文化语用能力。

（3）从本质看，课堂可以变得更以学生为中心、更有互动性。小组作业要求学生轮流扮演说话者和听话者的话语角色,不同的任务也让学生涉身不同的言语活动和交流活动。比如,角色扮演、模仿和话剧表演之类的活动,可能会使学生参与到不同的社会角色和言语活动之中。这些情景演练都是提供自然、真实的,包括附属语言信息的语言转换的绝佳条件。这些活动不仅可以展示出传统语言的种种生存发展境遇,也体现出了其某一特定的非言语手段和别的文化特征,就像合适的社会距离、目光语,等等。

(4)非母语英语情境中可以使用一种语用意识提升法来发展语用能力。这个方法使学习者去感知基于上下文使用语言的差异性,感知导致这些差异的因素,而不是教他们执行言语行为的具体方法。在非英语母语情境中,设置课堂背景、使用录像视频能帮助提升英语学习者的语用意识。课堂之外,英语老师可以举办有关英国文化、传统和历史等方面的演讲。应该给学生更多与英语外教交流的机会。通过和外教的互动,学生可以学到课堂上学不到的东西。

(5)中国英语教师应该努力了解两种语言的文化,或至少熟悉目标文化。仅仅解释字面意思和语言形式是远远不够的。最为重要的是,老师应该详细地解释出语言形式的不同语用功能,以及在不同情境中的用法。老师应该在教学过程中有意识的提出文化方面的观点。比如,教词汇时采用文化方面的资料,教学生新单词的内涵意义,把词汇按文化相关的群组分门别类,等等。教目标语文化时,老师不应仅仅给学生们灌输知识。更为重要的是,应该组织学生分组,对中英文化进行类比和比对。通过这种方式,学生们的文化敏感性和语用能力就能有所提升。

(6)必须对当前的语言考试系统进行改革。需要测试的不仅仅是学生的语言能力,还要测试他们相应的交际能力和语用能力。交际测试必须按照一些相当严格的标准进行,一定要对语法、话语、社会语言学、语用以及交际策略能力进行测试。测试一定要讲究实效,因为它要求学习者要自然而然地使用语言,进行真正意义上的交流,也要有思想、有感情。简言之,要在语境中使用地道的语言。它要测出学习者对各种语言功能的掌握。这样的测试会引导学生主动意识到(掌握)中英文化差异的重要性,两种语言中词汇术语的文化内涵的重要性,以及学习在不同场合如何恰当表现自己的重要性。

CHAPTER 6   CONCLUSION

So far, I have probed into the essence of pragmatic failures from three levels: firstly, from the level of pragmatic theories; secondly, from the level of practical experience; thirdly, from the level of test. It has been documented that pragmatic errors give rise to miscommunication.

Through careful analysis and study, I find that pragmatic failures are deeply rooted in the process of communication on the one hand; but on the other hand, they tend to be neglected and are not taken into serious consideration. I spend much space discussing and analyzing some pragmatic failures by virtue of some pragmatic theories. I hold that a large proportion of the phenomena of pragmatic failures can be explained and analyzed by these pragmatic theories.

According to Thomas, pragmatic failures are categorized into two types. The first type is pragmalinguistic failure, which is language-specific and caused by the inappropriate transfer of speech act strategies from one language to another. The other type is sociopragmatic failure, which is culture-specific and closely related to the culture difference between the mother language and the target language.

As far as pragmalinguistic failure is concerned, I believe that this kind of pragmatic failure belongs to the surface level of pragmatic failure and can be overcome under the proper guidance and instruction of teachers. On the other hand, sociopragmatic failure is at the deep level, which results from the corresponding differences in worldviews, cultural values and cultural surroundings.

I offer many examples associated with pragmalinguistic failures and sociolinguistic failures and give some detailed analysis for them as well. Through these examples and analysis, I go into some underlying reasons for these pragmatic failures. The first reason is that EFL learners usually pay much attention to the surface value of the utterances instead of inferring the underlying meaning. They are not sensitive to different contexts in making an utterance. The second reason is the negative transfer from the first language to the second language. The third reason is that the teaching of foreign language should be reasonable for the increasing of pragmatic failures. EFL teaching is falling behind the accelerative trend of intercultural communication. Both the teaching methodology and teaching materials are designed and chosen principally for the convenience of grammar presentation rather than from the cultural and pragmatic perspective.

A test conducted by the author shows that a person's grammatical knowledge and linguistic competence are not in a positive proportion to his or her pragmatic competence. The result strengthens the argument that even if a person has a good command of knowledge in phonetics, grammar and vocabulary, he or she will not certainly achieve the goal in the process of intercultural communication. From the test we may draw a lesson that strong emphasis must be placed equally on the development of linguistic competence and pragmatic competence. In addition, a questionnaire shows that the Chinese EFL learners are in a dilemma most of the time: it is hard for them to keep balance between the linguistic competence and pragmatic competence because of the present situations — the test-oriented educational system and the relevant EFL teaching methodology and thinking.

Teaching methodology, college-English syllabus design and language testing should play the important role in cultivating and improving EFL learners' pragmatic competence. Our college-English syllabus should be designed to create conditions conducive to the development of learners' pragmatic competence and cross-cultural awareness. It is generally acknowledged that language testing should closely follow the trends in language teaching. In language teaching, the focus has gradually being shifted to communicative competence whereas in language testing, the focus still remains on grammatical competence. As for teaching methodology, EFL teachers should consciously reflect cultural perspectives in the course of teaching. In short, the development of EFL learners' pragmatic competence is not only a necessary but also an urgent task in language teaching.

第6章 结 论

语用失误的确贯穿于跨文化交际之中。学习者的语言能力与其语用能力并非成正比。从三个层面探究了语用失误的本质：首先是从语用理论层面；其次是语用能力层面；最后是测试层面。目前已经证明，语用失误导致交际失误。

经过细致分析和研究，笔者发现，一方面，语用错误在交际过程中根深蒂固，而另一方面，这些错误又常常被忽视，没有被认真对待。通过利用语用理论我们讨论和分析了一些语用错误。并且认为，大部分语用错误现象都能通过这些语用理论解释和分析清楚。

根据 Thomas 所说，语用失误可分为两种。第一种是语用语言错误，它和语言相关，是从一种语言转换成另一种语言时，采用不当言语行为策略导致。另一种是社交语用错误，和文化有关，并且和母语与目标与之间的文化差异有密切联系。

就语用语言错误而言，它属于表面语用错误，可以通过老师适当的引导和教导来克服。此外，社交语用错误就属于深层错误，由相应的世界观、文化观以及文化背景方面的差异导致。

上述许多例子都和语用语言错误和社会语言错误有关。从这些例子和分析可得导致语用错误的根本原因。第一个原因就是，非母语英语学习者常常更加注重话语的表面意义，而不主动推敲语言背后的含义。他们说话时对不同的语境也不敏感。第二个原因是从母语到目标语言的负迁移。第三个原因是，外语教学应为不断出现的语用失误负责。非母语英语教学落后于越来越普遍的跨文化交际趋势。教学方法和教学材料的设计和选取都为了方便语法教学呈现，没有从文化和语用角度出发。

一个人的语法知识和语言学能力与他（或她）的语用能力并不成正比。结果进一步证实了论证，一个人即使不熟练掌握语音学、语法和词汇知识，他（或她）也会在跨文化交际过程达到目的。我们从测试中吸取的教训是，对语言能力和语用能力的培养都必须同样注重。而且,中国的英语学习者很多时候都陷入了学习困境:他们很难找到语言能力和语用能力之间的平衡,这些都是因为目前以考试为中心的教育系统体系以及相关的非母语英语教学方法和教学思想。

教学方法、大学英语教学大纲和语言测试都在培养和提高非母语英语学习者的语用能力方面起重要作用。我们设计大学英语教学大纲,应创造能培养学习者的语用能力和跨文化意识的有利环境。众所周知,语言测试要紧跟语言教学趋势。在语言教学中,重心已逐渐向交际能力转移。但在语言测试中,重心还在语法能力上。就教学方法而言,非母语英语老师应该在教学过程中有意识地体现一些文化观点。简言之,培养非母语英语学习者的语用能力,在语言教学中不但很有必要,也是一件刻不容缓的任务。

参 考 文 献

[1] ADMAJIAN A. Linguistics: an introduction to language and communication[M]. Cambridge, Massachusetts: MIT Press, 1995.

[2] AUSTIN J L. How to do things with words[M]. Harvard: Harvard University Press, 1975.

[3] BACHMAN L. Fundamental considerations in language testing[M]. Oxford: Oxford University Press, 1990.

[4] BROWN H, DOUGLAS. Principles to language learning and teaching[M]. London: Prentice-Hall, Inc, 1980.

[5] BROWN P, LEVISON S. Politeness: some universals in language usage[M]. Cambridge: Cambridge University Press, 1987.

[6] BYRAM, MICHAEL, Karen R. Language teachers, politics and cultures[M]. Sydney: Multilingual Matters LTD, 1999.

[7] CHOMSKY N. Aspects of the theory of syntax[M]. Cambridge, Massachusetts: MIT Press, 1965.

[8] CLAIRE K. Language and culture [M]. New York: Oxford University Press, 1997.

[9] CONDON, JOHN C, FATHI Y. An introduction to intercultural communication[M]. Indianapolis: Bobbs-Merrill, 1975.

[10] COULTHARD M. An introduction to discourse analysis [M]. London: Longman Group Limited, 1985.

[11] DENG Y, LIU R. Language and culture [M]. Beijing: Foreign Language Teaching and Research Press, 1989.

[12] FILMORE C. Santa cruz lectures on deixis[M]. Bloomington: IU Linguistic club, 1975.

[13] GAO Y. Understanding and transcending linguistic and cultural differences[M]. Beijing: Foreign Language Teaching and Research Press, 2000.

[14] GRICE P. Logic and conversation[M]. Oxford: Oxford University

Press，2009.

[15]　GUDYKUNST W B. Intercultural communication theory［M］. Beverly Hills，CA：Sage，1984.

[16]　HADLEY，ALICE，OMAGGIO. Teaching language in context［M］. Boston：Heinle & Heinle Publishers，1993.

[17]　HALLIDAY M A K. Language as social semiotic［M］. London：Edward Arnold Ltd，1978.

[18]　HANVEY，ROBERT G. Cross-cultural awareness，In Toward internationalism：readings in cross-cultural communication［C］. ed. By Elise C. Smith & Louise Fiber Luce，Newbury Publishers，Inc，1979.

[19]　HE Z. A new introduction to pragmatics［M］. Shanghai：Shanghai Foreign Language Educational Press，2000.

[20]　HE Z. Pragmatics and English learning［M］. Shanghai：Shanghai Foreign Language Educational Press，1997.

[21]　HU W. Culture and communication［M］. Beijing：Foreign Language Teaching and Research Press，1994.

[22]　HYMES D. On communicative competence［C］. In J. B. Pride & J. Holmes （ Eds.)， Sociolinguistics. Harmondsworth：Penguin Book，1972.

[23]　LEECH G. Principles of pragmatics［M］. London：Longman，1983.

[24]　LEVINSON，STEPHEN C. Pragmatics［M］. Beijing：Foreign Language Teaching and Research Press，2001.

[25]　MEY J. Pragmatics：an introduction［M］. Beijing：Foreign Language Teaching and Research Press，2001.

[26]　MILLER G. Between people［M］. Chicago：Science Research Associates，1974.

[27]　PECCEI J S. Pragmatics［M］. Beijing：Foreign Language Teaching and Research Press，2000.

[28]　PORTER E. An overview of intercultural communication. Selected Readings in Intercultural Communication［C］. ed. Hu，Wenzhong.

Changsha: Hunan Educational Press, 1990.

[29] SAMOVER L, PORTER, STEFANI L. A. Communication between cultures [M]. Beijing: Foreign Language Teaching and Research Press, 2000.

[30] SEARLE J R. Speech acts[M]. Cambridge: CUP, 1994.

[31] TRUDGILL P. Sociolinguistics: an introduction to language and society[M]. Harmondsworth: Penguin Books Ltd, 1982.

[32] VERSCHUEREN J. Understanding pragmatics[M]. Beijing: Foreign Language Teaching and Research Press, 2000.

[33] WARDHAUGH R. An introduction to sociolinguistics[M]. Oxford: Blackwel Publisher Ltd, 1996.

[34] WIDDOWSON H G. Teaching language as communication [M]. Oxford: Oxford University Press, 1989.

[35] WIDDOWSON H G. Explorations in applied linguistics[M]. Oxford: Oxford University Press, 1976.

[36] YULE G. Pragmatics [M]. Shanghai: Shanghai Foreign Language Educational Press, 2000.

[37] BARDOVI - HARLIG K, HARTFORD B S. Congruence in native and nonnative conversations: Status balance in the academic advisingsession[J]. Language learning, 1990(40): 467 - 501.

[38] CANALE M, SWAIN M. Theoretical bases of communicative approaches to second language learning andtesting [J]. Applied linguistics, 1980(1):58 - 59.

[39] CLENNEL C. Promoting pragmatic awareness and spoken discourse skills with EAPclasses[J]. ELT journal, 1999(2):53.

[40] TANG J L. Pragmatic failures and what they can tell us[J]. Teaching English in China, 2002,25(3):50 - 53.

[41] TRARONE E. Communication strategies, foreigner talk and repair in Interlanguage[J]. Language Learning, 1980(30): 417 - 431.

[42] THOMAS J. Cross-cultural pragmatic failure [J]. Applied Linguistics, 1983(6): 91 - 112.

［43］　胡文仲.跨文化交际面面观［M］. 北京:外语教学与研究出版社,2003.

［44］　钱冠连.汉语文化语用学［M］. 北京:清华大学出版社,2002.

［45］　何自然.语用学概论［M］.长沙:湖南教育出版社,1988.

［46］　夏纪梅.英语交际常识［M］.广州:中山大学出版社,1995.

［47］　贾玉新.跨文化交际学［M］.上海:上海外语教育出版社,1997.

［48］　徐余龙.对比语言学概论［M］.上海:上海外语教育出版社,1992.